PRAISE FOR

PRAYING THE BIBLE
THE BOOK OF PRAYERS

Many Christians struggle for years over how to pray effectively,
not realizing that the best prayers ever prayed can be found in God's
Word, the Bible. Wesley and Stacey Campbell demonstrate
how we can incorporate these into our own prayer lives and
reach a new level of intimacy with God.

DR. BILL BRIGHT
FOUNDER AND CHAIRMAN, CAMPUS CRUSADE FOR CHRIST

I have prayed the Bible regularly for three years. *The Book of Prayers*
is great because it's easy to read and pray. I used to run out of prayers
when I had to find them myself in the Bible. Now I can find them
way easier. This will make me pray more!

JUDAH CAMPBELL
TWELVE-YEAR-OLD SON OF WESLEY AND STACEY CAMPBELL

What a wonderful and timely book! For years I've longed to see
a compilation of practical, biblical prayers set forth in a simple way
to teach believers how to pray the Bible. No prayer is more powerful
than that which pleads God's promises. This marvelous book is
clearly a heaven-sent answer in response to that deep desire.

DR. DICK EASTMAN
INTERNATIONAL PRESIDENT, EVERY HOME FOR CHRIST

I love Wesley and Stacey's stuff. *The Book of Prayers* will equip youth everywhere with the resource needed to carry out this sweeping prayer revolution. I highly recommend this book!

LOU ENGLE
THE ELIJAH REVOLUTION AND THE CALL

As every church uses either hymnals or an overhead projector for worship, every intercessory ministry should use *The Book of Prayers* in their prayer rooms! We have waited for years for such a resource— finally it is here! A practical, inspiring tool to give you language to commune with God. Extraordinary!

JIM W. GOLL
MINISTRY TO THE NATIONS
AUTHOR, *EXODUS CRY*

The is one of the most valuable tools that intercessors could use for prayer.

CINDY JACOBS
PRESIDENT, GENERALS OF INTERCESSION
AUTHOR, *THE VOICE OF GOD* AND *DELIVER US FROM EVIL*

Praying the Bible has just gotten easier! *The Book of Prayers* shows how to pray the Bible through directions and examples missing from many other prayer books. A more intimate and close relationship with our Lord Jesus Christ awaits you. Read on!

DUTCH SHEETS
AUTHOR, *INTERCESSORY PRAYER*

The Book of Prayers will change your prayer life for eternity! And it will change you for eternity—and those for whom you pray. Jesus clearly instructed us to pray. Upon request, He gave an example of how to pray by praying the Word. The concept of praying the Scriptures is not new. The Shema "Hear, O Israel, the Lord your God, the Lord is one" was taught to ancient Hebrew children virtually as they learned to speak. We find throughout the Word examples of others who in their passionate pursuit of God's presence prayed the scriptural prayers of others before them. Wesley and Stacey Campbell are putting into your hands a powerful prayer tool, what they themselves call the "modern-day application of an ancient tradition." In chronological order, from Theophanies to Revelation, *The Book of Prayers* will set you on the pathway that leads to intimate relationship with the One who hears and answers every prayer.

TOMMY TENNEY
AUTHOR, *THE GOD CHASERS* AND *GOD'S DREAM TEAM*

Nothing could connect heaven and Earth more powerfully than praying God's Word. Wesley and Stacey Campbell's *The Book of Prayers* will guide you into this dynamic experience.

C. PETER WAGNER
CHANCELLOR, WAGNER LEADERSHIP INSTITUTE

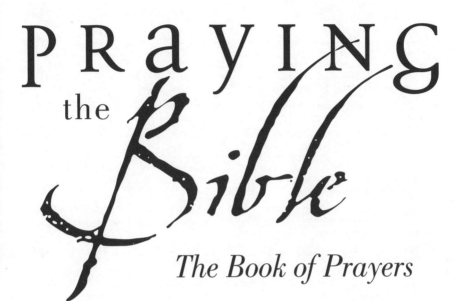

PRAYING
the
Bible

The Book of Prayers

WESLEY & STACEY
CAMPBELL

FOREWORD BY MIKE BICKLE

Regal

From Gospel Light
Ventura, California, U.S.A.

Published by Regal Books
From Gospel Light
Ventura, California, U.S.A.
Printed in the U.S.A.

Regal Books is a ministry of Gospel Light, an evangelical Christian publisher dedicated to serving the local church. We believe God's vision for Gospel Light is to provide church leaders with biblical, user-friendly materials that will help them evangelize, disciple and minister to children, youth and families.

It is our prayer that this Regal book will help you discover biblical truth for your own life and help you meet the needs of others. May God richly bless you.

For a free catalog of resources from Regal Books/Gospel Light, please call your Christian supplier or contact us at 1-800-4-GOSPEL *or* www.regalbooks.com.

Cover and interior design by Robert Williams
Edited by Amy Simpson

Library of Congress Cataloging-in-Publication Data
Campbell, Wesley.
    The book of prayers / Wesley & Stacey Campbell.
        p. cm.
Includes bibliographical references.
    ISBN 0-8307-3067-2 (trade paper)
    1. Bible—Prayers.   I. Campbell, Stacey.   II. Title.
    BS680.P64 C37 2002
    242'.722—dc21   2002006501

    3   4   5   6   7   8   9   10   11   12   13   14   15 / 09   08   07   06   05   04

Rights for publishing this book in other languages are contracted by Gospel Light Worldwide, the international nonprofit ministry of Gospel Light. Gospel Light Worldwide also provides publishing and technical assistance to international publishers dedicated to producing Sunday School and Vacation Bible School curricula and books in the lan-guages of the world. For additional information, visit www.gospellightworldwide.org; write to Gospel Light Worldwide, P.O. Box 3875, Ventura, CA 93006; or send an e-mail to info@gospellightworldwide.org.

DEDICATION

To Mike Bickle,

who first taught me to pray the Bible, and is now
inspiring the world to pray in International Houses of
Prayer (IHOPs) everywhere.

CONTENTS

Section One—Theophanies

*Paraphrased Scripture prayer.

Section Two—The Psalms

*Paraphrased Scripture prayer.

Section Three—Prayers of Wisdom

Section Four—The Song of Songs

Section Five—Prayers of the Prophets

*Paraphrased Scripture prayer.

Section Six—The Prayers of Jesus

*Paraphrased Scripture prayer.

Section Seven—Apostolic Prayers

*Paraphrased Scripture prayer.

Section Eight—Hymns of the Revelation

*Paraphrased Scripture prayer.

prayer

prayer is peace

FOREWORD

In 1979, the Lord called me to be an intercessor. Up until that time, I could count on one hand the hours I had spent in intercession. The entire concept was a mystery to me. What was intercession? How was I to do it? What good was it? For some time I fumbled around trying to figure out how to obey God in this new thing that He was calling me to do.

I finally realized that if I were going to pray at all, it would happen in real time and space. With that insight, I promptly scheduled 15 prayer meetings every single week, all with different groups of people, so that I would actually show up! Though we were faithful, I soon felt that this was not getting us anywhere. The meetings were flat and aimless, and we weren't all that joyful about being there. There had to be a better way.

Then I thought, *Why not copy out the prayers of Paul and pray those?* Excited with my new idea, I gathered up some white lined paper and scribbled out (in my own handwriting) a few of the apostolic prayers. The next day when the group showed up, I had photocopies of the various New Testament apostolic prayers for everyone. I was anxious to try out my new method. I held up one of Paul's prayers and haltingly read it out loud to

God. Everyone just looked at me. Then I said to the others, "Now it's your turn. Take one and pray it!" Somehow, we made it through the first week, to the next and then the next. Thus began the daily regimen of praying Bible prayers. We eventually grew into doing this three times a day for over seven years.

From those humble beginnings 20 years ago, God has brought forth a movement that emphasizes praying the Bible, which is a key value in our International House of Prayer of Kansas City (IHOP-KC). At the IHOP-KC, we offer up to Jesus worship and intercession 24 hours a day, 365 days a year. Trained and committed prayer missionaries fill 84 two-hour blocks of prayer each week, complete with prayer leaders, worship teams, sound crews and the rank-and-file intercessors. The main activity in every house of prayer is praying the Bible.

All this to say, "I rejoice to see Wesley and Stacey's new resource, *The Book of Prayers*." When I first met Wesley in 1989, he said he came to our annual conference because he struggled with prayer. As he learned to pray, the Lord put it on Wesley's heart to help others learn as well. This book is the fruit of that desire. Since those early days, Wesley and Stacey have also pioneered a whole new expression of biblical devotions with the *Praying the Bible* CDs. They have learned that when you give people the prayers, you give them the words which unlock their hearts. When Jesus' disciples asked Him to teach them to pray, He gave them a prayer which has unlocked the hearts of multitudes.

As an advocate of regularly praying the Bible, it's encouraging to see this old concept served up in a modern format. By arranging the prayers into eight distinct genres, every user will have instant access to whichever one he or she wants. The teaching behind the concept of praying the Bible out loud to God every day and the brief introductions at the beginning of each section help even the newest Christians understand how to make these prayers work for them. Prayer titles and page numbers make it possible for large gatherings to pray in an organized corporate fashion—that is, everyone can pray the same passage with the same translation for an extended period of time.

The Book of Prayers is the prayer devotional you have been waiting for. Every church and every prayer room should have plenty of copies. Pastors everywhere can mobilize their congregations to pray Bible prayers through this easy-to-use tool. I encourage parents to gather their families and pray these prayers with their children. I guarantee that if you pray *The Book of Prayers*, first, your communion with God will change; then, your life will change; and in the course of time, the whole world will change.

Mike Bickle
Founder, International House of Prayer of Kansas City
www.fotb.com

PREFACE

Prayer books are not new. As long ago as the time of Christ, the Jews had a body of prayers that were passed on through oral tradition. After the destruction of Jerusalem and the Temple and the Jews' final dispersion in 70 A.D., they were in danger of losing their prayer tradition. As a result, the Jews developed their own official book of prayers. At the same time, the Church was developing a tradition of prayer books with its own distinct prayer culture. Centuries later, circa 550 A.D., the Celtic church developed a pocket book version of Psalms that doubled as a prayer book. Subsequently, small prayer books flourished everywhere. In the days of the Reformation and beyond, the Protestant church developed their own *Common Book of Prayers*. Since then, virtually every branch of the Church has used prayer books.

Obviously, there is a pragmatic reason for all of the prayer books over the last 2,000 years, and that reason is, they work! People don't do things that don't work. And because most people don't pray as well as they want to, they look for help. The experts, the ones who really do it, realize that to pray well they need not only words, but words that have substance in their content. Without the words—the prayers—most people cannot maintain momentum in intercession and soon fall silent. When they grow silent, their minds wander, and by the time they realize it, they find themselves a million miles away from effective prayer. So, to help believers, the Church has always used prayer books.

The Book of Prayers attempts to give a new face to an old concept. The old concept is a prayer book. The new face is that the prayers have been laid out in eight distinct genres. Short introductions have been prepared for each prayer genre to assist children and novices, as well as seasoned intercessors, to stay focused in prayer. Altogether, there are 88 prayers directly from the Bible.

In *The Book of Prayers*, we have attempted to paraphrase the texts as little as possible. In the past, prayer books have often paraphrased the Bible beyond recognition or strung together small sections of Scripture according to topic so that the person praying was not able to pray one complete text. Other prayer books contain the prayers of famous saints through the ages. It's not that we disdain these excellent efforts, but the difference here is that we have extracted the actual biblical prayers and presented the scriptural texts in their entirety. A title has been assigned to each prayer, certain words have been either italicized or boldfaced for added emphasis and care has been taken in the placement and spacing of the verses so that the layout naturally leads the one praying. The only exception to this pattern is in the section entitled "Prayers of Wisdom." Here, the didactic nature of the literature requires verses to be gathered together and laid out in topical fashion, with a minimal amount of paraphrasing, in order to connect the thoughts or shape the text into a "prayable" prayer.

The prayers themselves are taken almost exclusively from the *New International Version* of the Bible. There are a few exceptions to this, one being "The Prayer of Jabez," which is referenced from the *New King James Version* due to the popularity of the prayer in the book of the same title. As mentioned earlier, paraphrasing has been kept to a bare minimum, but there are cases where a phrase or a word has been altered or added so that the prayer is easier to pray or more relevant to the modern reader. In some cases, a name is deleted or a space for your own name is provided. Occasionally, we have changed distinctly Old Testament concepts into New Testament equivalents. Examples of this would be "temple" changed to "kingdom" in the "Wholehearted Devotion" prayer, and "sacrifices of bulls" and "burnt offerings" changed to "true worship" in "A Prayer of Repentance." For "The Lord's Prayer," due to its sheer notoriety, we have used an adaptation of various translations, including the *New King James Version*, in order to form a composite of many versions. Of course, concerned intercessors can write their own notes and alterations into *The Book of Prayers* themselves, but it is hoped that the slight changes to the text are more helpful than bothersome.

Allowances must also be made for the fact that some of these prayers are over 3,000 years old. The accepted norm of writing in ancient times was to speak from a patriarchal, or male, perspective. We have left the text as it was written, but this is not meant to offend or belittle the female users. We judged that the transliterating of gender would have proved onerous to the intercessors themselves. In the case of the "Prayers of Wisdom," one must be sensitive to the style of writing, particularly in the male and female designations (i.e. "adulteress" and "wisdom," which are female; and "fool" and "king," which are male). It is assumed that both men and women will naturally allow for gender application, whether it is a woman praying the "Prayers of Wisdom," or men assuming the feminine bridal role in "The Song of Songs." Readers must make the gender translation, not allowing a gender-specific word to be an obstacle.

It must also be noted that my wife and I have written and produced the book together. Therefore, in the few instances when the word "I" is used, or an illustration is given from the perspective of one and not the other, this should be set in the context of the whole. That is, the whole was worked on by both of us, even though a few of the experiences are recorded as being singular.

The goal of *The Book of Prayers* was to bring the main Bible prayers all together in a single volume, which would be small and functional. The introductory sections render the book self-explanatory for even the newest disciple. Parents who have wanted their children to memorize Scripture will now be able to hand them *The Book of Prayers* and say, "Don't just memorize it, pray it!" We hope that *The Book of Prayers* becomes a working prayer book for intercessors and prayer rooms everywhere.

Bless you,
Wesley and Stacey Campbell

INTRODUCTION

Those who have determined in their hearts to develop a relationship with God will ultimately be driven to the place of prayer. There is no way around it. In the Bible, the greatest men and women of the Spirit were men and women of prayer. According to Scripture, Elijah was a man just like us, and he prayed earnestly that it would not rain on the land for three and a half years. Again he prayed and the heavens gave rain, and the earth produced its crops (see Jas. 5:17). Think about that. Elijah was a man just like you! When he prayed, it stopped raining for three and a half years, a dead boy was raised, and fire came down from heaven. He communicated with God in a manner that most Christians know nothing about. Noah and Abraham also bowed down to God. Jacob said, "Surely the LORD is in this place" (Gen. 28:16), so he set up an altar where he called upon God. Jacob wrestled with the angel of the Lord throughout the night (see Gen. 32:22-32). Moses spent days and nights in prayer. The record says that he went daily to the tent of the Lord, and Joshua went with him and stayed longer (see Exod. 33:7-11)! Samuel prayed. David wanted to gaze on God's beauty every day of his life (see Ps. 27:4). He cried out to the Lord morning, noon and night (see Ps. 55:17) and meditated on God "through the watches of the night" (Ps. 63:6). Daniel was in the practice of praying three times every day (see Dan. 6:10). It is a serious error to gloss over the prayer lives of the patriarchs of our faith, thinking we can imitate their works apart from imitating their prayer lives.

Our most striking prayer example, however, is Jesus Himself. How incredible that the perfect God-man seems to pray more than anyone else. He is always praying, and He instructs us to pray always (see Luke 18:1). In one sense, this is confusing. Why did Jesus, the God-man, have to pray so much? If anybody should be exempt from prayer, it would be Him. Yet He lived His life as though it really mattered that He prayed! In fact, nearly every chapter in the Gospel of Luke shows Jesus praying. Luke records that from the beginning of His public ministry Jesus prayed. "When all the people were being baptized, Jesus was baptized too. And as he was praying, heaven was opened" (Luke 3:21). This one statement, "as he was praying, heaven was opened," expresses the ministry of Jesus. Immediately following this prayer, Jesus is driven by the Spirit into the wilderness, where again He enters into prayer, complete with fasting, for 40 days (see Mark 1:12-13; Luke 4:1-2).

As news about Jesus spread, crowds came to hear Him and be healed of their sicknesses. What was Jesus' response to this? He "often withdrew to lonely places and prayed" (Luke 5:16). The optimum word here is "often"! Prayer for Jesus was not a once-in-a-while thing. He prayed regularly and consistently, and He would even spend whole nights in prayer. Before calling His disciples, "Jesus went out to a mountainside to pray, and spent the night praying to God" (Luke 6:12). His prayer life was so dynamic that He experienced dramatic manifestations. While He prayed, His face and clothes changed their appearance (see Luke 9:28-29) and sweat fell to the ground like great drops of blood (see Luke 22:44). He groaned, cried loudly and wept during His times of intercession (see Heb. 5:7). He got up early and stayed up late, just to pray (see Mark 1:35-38). Further, Jesus maintained that Temple life was all about prayer. "'It is written,' he said to them, '"My house will be a house of prayer"; but you have made it "a den of robbers"'" (Luke 19:46). He prayed for His disciples, and He prayed for us (see John 17:9,20). Jesus was always praying.

Why did He do this? Did Jesus know something we don't? Did He understand that spiritual authority, even His own, came through prayer, because prayer is the mechanism that produces a relationship with the Father? Did Jesus really believe that He could do nothing by Himself? Did He know that if He did not pray, there would be no mighty works? Perhaps He understood that He could receive more words, more power and more authority to do the Father's will if He prayed? He also seemed to instinctively know when it was time to withdraw and pray (see Luke 5:16). Because of this, the work He was called to do never distracted Him from His source of power for the work.

Those who were closest to Jesus recognized that there was something different about the way He prayed, so they asked Him to teach them how to pray. "Lord, teach us to pray, just as John taught his disciples" (Luke 11:1). Gladly, Jesus responded. In essence, He told the disciples to always pray and never give up (see Luke 18:1); to watch and pray so that they would not fall into temptation (see Matt. 26:41). God also directs you to go into your closet alone and pray in secret so that the Father who sees you in secret will reward you (see Matt. 6:6). Frankly, every Christian must come to terms with the fact that Jesus, as well as

Moses, Daniel, David, Elijah, John the Baptist and the rest, actually practiced continual prayer, and because of this, they had more power and authority than anyone else. How can we see the direct correlation between their consistent prayer lives and the great power and authority they walked in and not be inspired to imitate their example?

After 20 years of full-time Christian work, we are convinced that the reason most people do not pray is not because they are fundamentally disobedient or unspiritual—it's just that they don't know how. For my part, I spent the better part of a decade trying to teach myself how to pray and get others praying as well. This prayer book is the distillation of 12 years of trying to learn how to pray.

My first discovery was that people in every place and at every time have prayed the Bible. It was shocking to find that for thousands of years godly men and women had used the model of praying the Bible—out loud—to God—every day! Virtually every denomination of the Church has done this. From the starting point of praying the Bible out loud, many have moved into advanced stages of silent or infused prayer. Yet everyone learns to walk before they run. To reach the mountaintop of silent prayer, one must first climb the various plateaus of vocal prayer. In time, we will naturally move into places of silence. However, the starting place for Jews and Christians has always been the same—praying the Bible out loud. It might even be said that modern-day evangelical/charismatic Christianity is the first generation of the people of God in over 3,000 years to not do prayer right!

When we look deeper into the prayer life of Jesus, we discover some interesting patterns. We know that Jesus was Jewish, and as a Jew, He was brought up according to custom (see Luke

2:22,42; 4:16). What most modern readers don't know is that the Jewish custom of prayer was very defined in Jesus' day. It originated in the first books of the Old Testament and was based on a very literal understanding of the Scriptures. The first major commandment on prayer is found in the greatest of all Jewish commandments, the Shema.

> Hear, O Israel: The LORD our God, the LORD is one. Love the LORD your God with all your heart and with all your soul and with all your strength. These commandments that I give you today are to be upon your hearts. Impress them on your children. Talk about them when you sit at home and when you walk along the road, when you lie down and when you get up. Tie them as symbols on your hands and bind them on your foreheads. Write them on the doorframes of your houses and on your gates (Deut. 6:4-9).

According to the Babylonian Talmud, Jewish boys were taught this passage as soon as they could speak (*Sukkah 42a*).[1] It further specifies that "the *father* must teach him."[2] Therefore, it is safe to assume that Joseph taught his son, Jesus, how to pray this passage. In fact, the Shema is central to the whole of Jewish life. In his classic work *To Be a Jew*, Rabbi Donin writes:

> To engage in prayer is the most obvious and the most universal reflection of man's relationship with God. Prayer in its highest form and at its most sincere levels is called a "service of the heart," and constitutes one of the many ways by which love of God is expressed.[3]

As you can see, for every Jew, the Shema was a call to prayer. And prayer, according to the Rabbis, was a proof of one's love for God. Simply put, the first of the Ten Commandments, to worship the LORD your God (see Exod. 20:1-6; Deut. 5:6-10); the Shema, "Love the LORD your God" (Deut. 6:5); and the oft-repeated commandment "to serve the LORD your God" (Deut. 10:12; see 11:13) are all fulfilled by prayer. Prayer becomes at once the means and proof of love. This tradition of prayer as a service of the heart was the Jewish tradition that Jesus was raised in.

Tradition would have also dictated that Jesus pray every day. Throughout the Bible, we see that the people of God prayed day and night, continuously and without ceasing. Of course, the obvious question is whether God is really serious about having His people pray day and night. What do *day* and *night* really mean? Is it just a religious cliché? How Israel understood Deuteronomy 6:4-13 and Joshua 1:8 is evidenced by how they lived out those verses. When Zechariah went into the holy of holies and "the time for the burning of incense came, all the assembled worshipers were praying outside" (Luke 1:10). How early this practice started we cannot know, but when Moses would go into the tent of meeting to talk to God, all of the Israelites worshiped at the entrance of their own tents (see Exod. 33:8-10). By the time of David, we know that morning and evening prayers had become the norm within Tabernacle/Temple worship. David said, "But I call to God and the LORD saves me. Evening, morning and noon, I cry out in distress, and he hears my voice" (Ps. 55:16-17). David's prescribed pattern in the Temple was to have morning and evening prayer.

Since David believed the sacrifices should be accompanied with morning and evening prayers, he stated, "The duty of the Levites was to help Aaron's descendants in the service of the temple of the LORD. . . . They were also to stand every morning to thank and praise the LORD. They were to do the same in the evening" (1 Chron. 23:28,30). Daniel carried this practice to the point of obsession as a captive in Babylon, where under threat of death he refused to break his habit of praying three times daily. "Three times a day he got down on his knees and prayed, giving thanks to his God, just as he had done before" (Dan. 6:10). Historians tell us that sometime after the 70 years of captivity in Babylon (c. 450 B.C.), Ezra determined that Israel would never again provoke God to such wrath. So he mandated daily prayers, accompanied by readings from the Torah. In time, it became the custom for Jews to pray the 18 *Benedictions*, coupled with readings from the Torah, over three set hours of prayer at the Temple, synagogue or home. This custom was firmly in place long before the birth of Jesus. Accordingly, Jesus, along with every righteous Jew, would have observed this practice daily. It is interesting to think that Jesus, His father Joseph and Joseph's father all would have prayed this way; that Peter, James and John grew up praying set prayers every day; and that Paul was steeped in the model of Jewish prayer.

The evidence from the New Testament is that *day* and *night* prayer times were observed by the Early Church, as well as by the God-fearers who had attached themselves to Judaism. Luke records, "One day Peter and John were going up to the temple *at the time of prayer* [the ninth hour]" (Acts 3:1, emphasis added). Cornelius, a Gentile God-fearer, is called a devout man who prayed continually (see Acts 10:2). The following verses explain what continual prayer means:

About the ninth hour of the day, *the hour of prayer*, Cornelius clearly saw in a vision an angel of God who came to him and said to him, "Cornelius! Your prayers and alms have ascended as a memorial before God" (see Acts 10:2-4, emphasis added).

Hourly prayer is further implied when Peter goes up to his rooftop to pray at the *noon time of prayer* (see Acts 10:9). The outpouring of Pentecost happened at nine in the morning, the third hour, also a time of prayer (see Acts 2:15). It says of the Early Church born at Pentecost that those who believed were daily (and continually) in the Temple courts, as well as meeting in the homes of believers (see Luke 24:53; Acts 2:46). What did they do daily in the Temple courts? Jesus said they prayed. With fury He demanded, "My house [the Temple] will be called a house of prayer for all nations" (Mark 11:17) and earlier described how "Two men went up to the temple to pray" (Luke 18:10). The Early Church was not celebrating or gossiping in the Temple courts. They were praying daily and continually, fulfilling the customary hours of prayer.

As you can see, both the Jews and the Early Church prayed a minimum of three set times per day. The first hour ranged from 6:00 A.M. to 9:00 A.M., the second was at noon and the third somewhere between 3:00 P.M. and 6:00 P.M. Whether they felt like it or not, whether they knew how to do it or not, whether they felt inspired or not, as worshipers of God, they were just called to show up and pray. Jesus and the apostles did this, and like them, we are called to do it as well. Like them, we need to set a time and make a place to get face-to-face with God.

The other practice of Jesus was that He *prayed the Bible*. The Jews had a body of prayers that everyone prayed, which had been passed on through oral tradition. These prayers were all based on the Law of God, which God gave us from the beginning. Joshua was told specifically to *"meditate on it* [the Book of the Law] day and night" (Josh. 1:8, emphasis added). David put this into practice, and we got the Psalms (see Ps. 1:2). The prophets did it, and we got the Prophetic Books. Ultimately, the expansion of the Law, the book of Psalms and the Prophetic Books make up what Jesus deemed to be the Scriptures (see Luke 24:27,44). These are the Words that have been given to us to pray. Paul put it this way, "This is what we speak, not in words taught us by human wisdom but in words taught by the Spirit, expressing spiritual truths in spiritual words" (1 Cor. 2:13). The entire Bible is God breathed—it is the language of the Spirit; it is the language of prayer.

Throughout history, the Church has taught the faithful to pray by praying the Bible. No denomination of the Church has ever questioned this time-honored method. As far back as our Judaistic roots, and on into the New Testament times, during the age of the Desert Fathers and throughout recent Church history, the saints and all believers were taught to pray the Bible. Virtually every famous Christian through the ages has preached and practiced praying the Bible.

Thus, *The Book of Prayers* becomes the modern-day application of an ancient tradition. The genres of prayer are laid out in chronological order, just as they appear in the Bible. They are:

- Theophanies
- The Psalms
- Prayers of Wisdom
- The Song of Songs

- Prayers of the Prophets
- The Prayers of Jesus
- Apostolic Prayers
- Hymns of the Revelation

Also, in order to facilitate effective prayer, a detailed description of how to pray each section is provided in its introduction. This prayer book continues the practice that even Jesus Himself did—the praying of the Law back to God.

Lastly, when Jesus prayed the Bible, He did it out loud. Hebrews 5:7 says, "During the days of Jesus' life on earth, he offered up prayers and petitions with loud cries and tears . . . and he was heard because of his reverent submission." Does this mean that we have to cry bitterly and pray loudly in order to be heard? The obvious answer is no! But the not-so-obvious implication is that we cannot cry or pray loudly unless we are deeply immersed in what we are doing. Jesus was emotionally engaged when He prayed. He was wholly taken over by His prayer. He was sweating and weeping because He was praying so intensely (see Luke 22:44).

I am often in the habit of asking people a semi-trick question—do you know why God wants you to pray the Bible out loud? After I ask this question, people tend to look at one another questioningly. Pausing for dramatic effect, I reply: So you know when you've stopped! This usually takes a moment to sink in and then they all begin to snicker at one another. If you think about it for a moment, you will see the simple wisdom of this statement. It is hard to think about something other than what you're talking about. Praying out loud solves the problem of the wandering mind. The Desert Father St. Cassian said, "The man who prays only when on his knees, prays little. The man who kneels to pray and then lets his mind wander, prays not at all."[4] In Joshua 1:8, an antidote for the malady of the wandering mind is prescribed in the very Word given by God when He commanded the Israelites to pray. That word is "meditate." But unfortunately, most of us wrongly interpret "to meditate" as something we do silently. Even worse, some understand it only in the context of Eastern religions, where it implies the emptying of one's self to achieve nirvana, or nothingness. All of this is a gross misunderstanding of what the word "meditate" means. *Strong's* definition of the Hebrew word for "meditate," which is *hagah*, means "to imagine, meditate, mourn, mutter, roar, speak, study, talk, utter."[5] *The International Standard Bible Encyclopaedia* interprets it as "to murmur, to have a deep tone, to sigh, moan," or *higgayon*, "the murmur or dull sound of the harp."[6] This is biblical meditation.

In the Bible, equivalents of "hagah" are as follows: the lion roars or growls (hagah) over his prey (see Isa. 31:4); we moan (hagah) like doves (see Isa. 59:11); and mediums and spiritists whisper and mutter (hagah) (see Isa. 8:19). From these contexts, we discern that "hagah" (meditate) meant "to say over and over again, to speak, to mutter, to recite, to expel air out loud." There was to be physical involvement in this activity. And in the case of Joshua, he was to hagah—to say over and over again—the Book of the Law out loud to God.

Obviously, when this command was given to ancient Israel, they didn't have many copies of the Law. Unlike today, the average Israelite family would not have had their own personalized scroll of the Book of the Law. So how could they obey that command? Through oral recitation they learned to meditate on the Law. One can only imagine the early Israelites gathering in groups to chant the Law. The men would later pass on what they learned to their families at home (see Deut. 6:4-13). That is why every letter of the Hebrew Scriptures is set to musical notations, or tropes, which make memorization possible and facilitate vocal meditation. Some of the psalms and proverbs are even structured in the style of musical acrostics (see Ps. 119; Prov. 31). It was almost like an ancient form of Hebrew rap, if you will. In this manner, they passed the Commandments on to their children and developed the power to do the Law itself. They prayed the Words out loud back to God until the Law took root in their hearts. To this very day, Jews pray out loud. We have all seen them at the Wailing Wall in prayer, bobbing and rocking as they mutter the Law. Their whole body is involved in meditation. It is not merely a mental exercise or a passive contemplation. No, it is an engaging recitation of a specific text addressed to the Lord. One could say that they used their mouths—to lasso their minds—to affect their spirits.

All of this may sound strange to nontraditional ears. However, if the truth were known, the modern Islamic practice of praying five times a day—by reciting scriptures out loud while facing Mecca (instead of Jerusalem)—is closer to New Testament prayer than we think. In fact, the five pillars of Islam: statement of faith, daily prayer (five times a day), almsgiving, fasting and pilgrimage to their holy site, were all modeled after common and prevalent practices of the Church at that time (seventh century A.D.). The sad thing is that the prayer practice Muslims learned from Christianity, and often practice out of legalism, Christians will not practice out of love. But the fact remains that the pathway to intimacy with God is found in praying the Bible. That is why every family needs to be intent on praying the Bible—out loud—to God—every day!

prayer is peace

THEOPHANIES

In the thirtieth year, while I was among the exiles by the Kebar River, the heavens were opened and I saw visions of God.

INTRODUCTION

What are the theophanies, and why begin *The Book of Prayers* with these selections of Scripture? These two questions must be answered at the outset, as they greatly affect the way we pray. The Bible commands us to pray, to meditate and to recite the Law to God. Of course, people of every religion pray, and they all think they are praying to God. But who is right? Which god is the true God? Where is He? What is He like? What is He doing? These are questions that any worshiper will consider when he or she sets aside time to talk to God.

When speaking on the topic of prayer, I often ask a congregation to stand up so that I can give them a test. The question I give them is this: If you know the location of at least four of the many God sightings in the Bible, and you can generally recount what the prophet saw, then stay standing. At first people begin to look around, dumbfounded. Then, slowly, with sheepish, sideway glances, almost everyone begins to sit down. Rarely is even 3 percent of the audience left standing. Almost no one is in the regular practice of praying the theophanies, that is, the God sightings.

It is hard to overstate the seriousness of this spiritual omission. For instance, imagine if seven of the most holy, prophetically inspired men and women of all of Christendom made a pilgrimage to a mountain, where they fasted and prayed for a week for a breakthrough with God. Imagine that God actually came down in a full-blown, visible display of His glory. Imagine that these seven were overwhelmed and laid low in the awesome presence of God. Then, as soon as they were able, they came down and declared that they had seen God with their eyes and that they would be gathering at a specific time and place to tell about it. Who wouldn't want to be there? Who wouldn't want to read a detailed account?

Yet we have the greatest holy men of history—men like Moses (see Exod. 24,34); Isaiah (see Isa. 6); Ezekiel (see Ezek. 1,10); Daniel (see Dan. 7,10); Peter (see Matt. 17); and John (see Rev. 1,4,19,21)—all of whom say they saw God (or the glorified Christ) with their eyes and wrote down what they saw. How absurd is it, then, for devoted believers who have given their whole lives to love and serve God, who say they believe in the inspiration and inerrancy of these accounts, to not even know where God sightings are found, much less be able to recite them in their minds and spirits?

The word "theophanies" derives its meaning from two Greek words: *theos* and *phaino*. *Theos* means "God" and *phaino* means "to appear or show"; hence, the "God appearances." The Old Testament narrates numerous times when the infinite, invisible God "shows up" in specific, "concrete" ways. God revealed Himself "right there" in front of people. God walked and talked with Adam and Eve in the cool of the day in the garden (see Gen. 3:8). He came upon Abraham as one of three traveling strangers (see Gen. 18:1,13). He showed Himself as an awesome King to Isaiah, complete with throne room, smoke and seraphic attendants (see Isa. 6:1-4). It is these instances and more that show us glimpses of where God lives and who is around Him and, to some extent, what He is doing. For instance, in Daniel 7:9-10, the "Ancient of Days" is sitting on His throne, judging in a courtroom setting; in Revelation 4, He is the center of a breathtaking scene in heaven, and we get a picture of those who are worshiping before His throne. In each case, the people who witnessed these things experienced the reality of the Divine One "up close and personal." They then prayed to God as He had revealed Himself.

As such, the theophanies are an ideal starting point for our prayers, because we also can pray to God as He has revealed Himself. Therefore, when you pray certain theophanies, you will discover that God is not just remote and far off but close and personal. With other theophanies, you will familiarize yourself with the sights, sounds and smells of heaven—you will "see" just who it is you are talking to. You will gain confidence that God really wants to hear your prayers and that you are addressing the One who has all power in heaven and Earth to answer. And, if you pray the theophanies long enough, your relationship with God will change. As you address Him as He reveals Himself, revelation will pour out of each one of His attributes. Intimacy and communion will flow between you and God as the Holy Spirit unveils God the Father and God the Son, revealing to us more and more of Christ each day.

When we pray the theophanies, we begin to touch His power, to hear that loud voice like many waters, to tremble in the presence of the thunders and lightning bolts. Any person who does not at some time pray the theophanies may limit God in their own thinking. To them, God may be experienced as smaller than He really is, because the person will be praying to God as they understand Him to be, not as He has revealed Himself to be. After all, God is who He says He is, not who we think He is! So, it is essential to begin all prayer by praying to God on a personal level. Praying the theophanies will keep us from praying to an extension of our own darkened minds.

Also, praying the theophanies will reveal that an entirely different world exists beyond this base plain on which we live. Yahweh has a heavenly council that convenes to discuss affairs on Earth (see Job 1; 1 Kings 22). The theophanies illustrate the multiple ranks of angels with magnificent powers, who surround God in heaven. All of these awesome beings have the capacity for independent thought and action. They offer their counsel and volunteer for service. They exist in a host of different levels with different functions, beauties and strengths. You will learn how this other world intersects with our world (see Dan. 10)—how it impacts it, moves it, changes it and communicates with it. Soon, like Elisha's servant, you will realize that more are they that are for us than those that are against us (see 2 Kings 6:16). Your faith will take on prophetic proportions. You will reach a whole new spiritual level when you repeatedly pray the theophanies.

That a fuller understanding of God will be gained by praying the theophanies is evidenced by examining the visions of Daniel. In Daniel 7, God appears to Daniel as an old man, revealing himself as the "Ancient of Days." We can only surmise, but perhaps God presents Himself as old in order to identify with Daniel in his old age. Interestingly, another figure, "one like a son of man" (Dan. 7:13), is also introduced at this point for the first time in Scripture. Daniel does not ascribe to Him the traditional "angel of the Lord" title (see Gen. 22:15; Judg. 6:11-24; 13:3). In fact, this mysterious second personality in Daniel seems to be described in terms that were previously reserved for God Himself. Initially, the "one like a son of man" comes in the clouds. In praying the theophanies, seasoned intercessors will know that if the clouds do not indicate divinity, then this would be the only exception in about 75 Old Testament passages in which clouds do accompany or symbolize divinity.[1] Of course, when Daniel wrote this, he would not have had a clear concept of the Incarnation that God had a Son who was pre-existent before He was incarnated as a human. And what is more all of this flew in the face of everything Daniel—a strict monotheist—thought he knew about "the LORD your God is One" (Deut. 6:4). Since Daniel did not completely understand this concept, all he could say was, "I did not understand" (Dan. 12:8), but he did know what he saw! It is only after Christ's birth, life, death, resurrection and ascension that all the pieces of revelation come together.

Even though Daniel does not understand all of what he sees and hears, the New Testament provides a fuller understanding of the mysterious angel of the Lord and of the One like a Son of Man. In the trial of Jesus,

> the high priest asked him, "Are you the Christ, the Son of the Blessed One?" "I am," said Jesus. "And you will see the Son of Man sitting at the right hand of the Mighty One and coming on the clouds of heaven." The high priest tore his clothes. "Why do we need any more witnesses?" he asked. "You have heard the blasphemy" (Mark 14:61-64).

Jesus Himself referred to the theophany in His trial to describe who He was, in and doing so, made a declaration of His divinity, ultimately causing His condemnation of death.

One of the most intriguing visions in the Old Testament is found in Daniel 10:5-6, where the sage sees a glorious "man dressed in linen." A careful study shows a remarkable correspondence to the words John used to describe Christ in Revelation 1:13-16. It is almost unimaginable that this glorious man is not the pre-incarnate Christ that John would see hundreds of years later on the Island of Patmos. Knowing full well the vision of Daniel, John chooses the exact words to describe his vision that Daniel used in his portrayal of the "man dressed in linen."

In Daniel 10–12, the glorious man, while on assignment "sent" from heaven, gives astonishingly accurate predictions of coming historical events—insights into spiritual warfare in the heavenlies between God and His mightiest angels over the demonic spirits of nations, and words of hope and comfort concerning the resurrection and eternal life. Who among us wouldn't be thrilled to have the privilege of receiving such revelation? Praying the theophanies will help open your eyes to these events and more.

From just this one example, it is evident how praying the theophanies will lead you to a much fuller understanding of the Godhead. The nuances are more than could fill a book. Practically, the way to pray the theophanies is to recite them out loud to God as they are written, until you are absolutely familiar with each encounter. Then, with a thorough understanding of each of the heavenly visions, begin to insert your own name in place of Daniel's, Ezekiel's, etc. You should imagine and believe that similar things are happening in the Spirit as you pray today, just as they were happening when the prophets prayed way back when. You may even change the name of the principality in the text to the names of those principalities over your own country—or over those for whom you are interceding. Like Daniel, we may not understand everything we see and pray, because the finite will never completely understand the infinite. However, we will be able to delve much deeper into the nature of God than if we had never meditated on these God sightings.

Coming full circle, the fact remains that praying the theophanies will reveal God in glimpses. And if men, women and especially children are ever going to pray effectively, they must first start by seeing Him. We must pray the theophanies until heaven becomes as familiar to us as our earthly homes. Our children should be able to close their eyes and see God sitting on the throne, envision the sea of glass and hear the living creatures in heaven, with all of the corresponding movement, color and sound. Imagine if we were able to mentally walk through the surroundings of heaven and have them be as familiar as our earthly surroundings. My advice to everyone is always the same: Both you and your children should begin to pray Revelation 4 at least 100 times out loud to God, 10 times a day, for 10 days straight. Then, you will see God! And since prayer is talking to God, a great place to begin is with the theophanies, because they show us who God really is.

Visions of God

In the thirtieth year,
in the fourth month on the fifth day,
while I was among the exiles by the Kebar River,
the heavens were opened and I saw visions of God.

There the hand of the LORD was upon me.

I looked,
and I saw a windstorm coming out of the north—
an immense cloud with flashing lightning
and surrounded by brilliant light.

The center of the fire looked like glowing metal,
and in the fire was what looked like *four living creatures.*
In appearance their *form* was that of a *man,*
but each of them had *four faces* and *four wings.*

Their *legs* were straight;
their *feet* were like those of a calf
and gleamed like burnished bronze.

Under their *wings* on their four sides
they had the **hands of a man.**
*All four of them had **faces** and **wings,***
and their wings touched one another.
Each one went straight ahead;
they did not turn as they moved.

Their faces looked like this:
Each of the four had the face of a *man,*
and on the right side each had the face of a *lion,*
and on the left the face of an *ox;*
each also had the face of an *eagle.*
Such were their faces.

Their wings were spread out upward;
each had two wings,
one touching the wing of another creature on either side,
and two wings covering its body.

Each one went straight ahead.
Wherever the spirit would go, they would go,
without turning as they went.

The appearance of the living creatures
was like burning coals of fire or like torches.
Fire moved back and forth among the creatures;
it was bright, and lightning flashed out of it.
The creatures sped back and forth like flashes of lightning.

As I looked at the living creatures,
I saw a wheel on the ground beside each creature
with its four faces.

This was the appearance and structure of the wheels:
They sparkled like chrysolite,
and all four looked alike.
Each appeared to be made like a wheel intersecting a wheel.

As they moved,
they would go in any one of the four directions
the creatures faced;
the wheels did not turn about as the creatures went.

Their rims were high and awesome,
and all four rims were ***full of eyes*** all around.

When the living creatures moved,
the wheels beside them moved;
and when the living creatures rose from the ground,
the wheels also rose.

Wherever the spirit would go,
they would go,
and the wheels would rise along with them,
because the spirit of the living creatures was in the wheels.

When the creatures moved, they also moved;
when the creatures stood still, they also stood still;
and when the creatures rose from the ground,
the wheels rose along with them,
because the spirit of the living creatures was in the wheels.

Spread out above the heads of the living creatures was what
looked like an expanse, sparkling like ice, and awesome.

Under the expanse their wings were stretched out
one toward the other,
and each had two wings covering its body.

When the creatures moved,
I heard the sound of their wings,
like the roar of rushing waters,
like the voice of the Almighty,
like the tumult of an army.
When they stood still,
they lowered their wings.

Then there came a voice
from above the expanse over their heads
as they stood with lowered wings.
Above the expanse over their heads
was what looked like a throne of sapphire,
and high above on the throne was a figure like that of a man.

I saw that from what appeared to be his waist up
he looked like glowing metal, as if full of fire,
and that from there down he looked like fire;
and brilliant light surrounded him.
Like the appearance of a rainbow in the clouds on a rainy day,
so was the radiance around him.

This was the appearance
of the likeness of the glory of the LORD.

When I saw it, I fell facedown,
and I heard the voice of one speaking.

Ezekiel 1:1,3-28

Yahweh and the Ten Commandments

On the morning of the third day
there was **thunder** and **lightning,**
with **a thick cloud** over the mountain,
and a very **loud trumpet** blast.
Everyone in the camp trembled.
Then Moses led the people out of the camp to meet with God,
and they stood at the foot of the mountain.

Mount Sinai was covered with **smoke,**
because the **LORD** descended on it in **fire.**
The **smoke billowed up** from it like smoke from a furnace,
the whole **mountain trembled** violently,
and the **sound** of the trumpet grew **louder and louder.**

Then Moses spoke and the **voice** of God answered him.
The **LORD** descended to the top of Mount Sinai
and called Moses to the top of the mountain.

The *LORD* replied,
"Go down and bring Aaron up with you.
But the priests and the people must not force their way through
to come up to the *LORD,* or he will break out against them."
So Moses went down to the people and told them.

And God spoke all these words:

"I am the LORD your God,
who brought you out of Egypt, out of the land of slavery.

"You shall have no other gods before me.

"You shall not make for yourself an idol
in the form of anything in heaven above or on the earth beneath
or in the waters below. You shall not bow down to them or
worship them; *for I, the LORD your God, am a jealous God,*
punishing the children for the sin of the fathers to the third
and fourth generation of those who hate me, but showing love
to a thousand generations of those who love me
and keep my commandments.

"You shall not misuse the name of the LORD your God,
for the **LORD** will not hold anyone guiltless who
misuses his name.

"Remember the Sabbath day by keeping it holy.
Six days you shall labor and do all your work, but the seventh
day is a Sabbath to the **LORD** your God. On it you shall not
do any work, neither you, nor your son or daughter, nor your
manservant or maidservant, nor your animals, nor the alien
within your gates. For in six days the **LORD** made the heavens
and the earth, the sea, and all that is in them, but he
rested on the seventh day. Therefore the **LORD** blessed the
Sabbath day and made it holy.

"Honor your father and your mother,
so that you may live long in the land the **LORD** your God is
giving you.

"You shall not murder.

"You shall not commit adultery.

"You shall not steal.

"You shall not give false testimony against your neighbor.

"You shall not covet your neighbor's house.
You shall not covet your neighbor's wife, or his
manservant or maidservant, his ox or donkey, or anything
that belongs to your neighbor."

When the people saw the **thunder** and **lightning**
and heard the **trumpet** and saw the **mountain** in **smoke,**
they trembled with fear.
They stayed at a distance and said to Moses,
"Speak to us yourself and we will listen.
But do not have God speak to us or we will die."

Moses said to the people,
"Do not be afraid. God has come to test you,
so that the fear of God will be with you
to keep you from sinning."

The people remained at a distance,
while Moses approached the thick darkness where God was.

Exodus 19:16-20,24-25; 20:1-21

SHOW ME YOUR GLORY

Then Moses said to him,
"If your Presence does not go with us,
do not send us up from here.
How will anyone know
that you are pleased with me
and with your people
unless you go with us?
What else will distinguish me and your people
from all the other people on the face of the earth?"

And the **LORD** said to Moses,
"I will do the very thing you have asked,
because I am pleased with you
and I know you by name."

Then Moses said,
"Now show me your glory."

And the **LORD** said,
"I will cause all my goodness
to pass in front of you,
and I will proclaim my name,
the LORD,
in your presence.
I will have mercy
on whom I will have mercy,
and I will have compassion
on whom I will have compassion."

Then the **LORD** came down in the cloud
and stood there with him
and *proclaimed His name,*
the LORD.

And he passed in front of Moses, proclaiming,

"The LORD,
the LORD, the compassionate and gracious God,
slow to anger,
abounding in love and faithfulness,
maintaining love to thousands,
and forgiving wickedness,
rebellion and sin.

"Yet he does not leave the guilty unpunished;
he punishes the children
and their children
for the sin of the fathers
to the third and fourth generation."

Moses bowed to the ground at once
and worshiped.

When Moses came down from Mount Sinai
with the two tablets of the Testimony in his hands,
he was not aware that his face was radiant
because he had spoken with the LORD.

Exodus 33:15-19; 34:5-8,29

———

EYES AND WINGS

I looked,
and I saw the likeness of a throne of sapphire
above the expanse that was over the heads of the **cherubim.**

The **LORD** said to the man clothed in linen,
"Go in among the wheels beneath the *cherubim.*
Fill your hands with burning coals from among the *cherubim*
and scatter them over the city."
And as I watched, he went in.

Now the *cherubim* were standing on the south side of the
temple when the man went in,
and a cloud filled the inner court.

Then the glory of the LORD rose from above the cherubim
and moved to the threshold of the temple.
The cloud filled the temple,
and the court was full of the radiance of the
glory of the LORD.

The sound of the wings of the *cherubim* could be heard
as far away as the outer court,
like the voice of *God Almighty* when he speaks.

When the **LORD** commanded the man in linen,
*"Take fire from among the **wheels,***
from among the *cherubim,"*
the man went in and stood beside a wheel.

Then one of the *cherubim* reached out his hand
to the fire that was among them.
He took up some of it and put it into the hands
of the man in linen,
who took it and went out.

(Under the wings of the *cherubim*
could be seen what looked like the hands of a man.)

I looked,
and I saw beside the *cherubim four wheels,*
one beside each of the cherubim;
the *wheels* sparkled like chrysolite.

As for their appearance,
the four of them looked alike;
each was like a wheel intersecting a wheel.

As they moved,
they would go in any one of the four directions
the *cherubim* faced;
the *wheels* did not turn about as the *cherubim* went.
The *cherubim* went in whatever direction the head faced,
without turning as they went.

Their entire bodies,
including their backs,
their hands and their wings,
were completely full of eyes,
as were their four wheels.

I heard the wheels being called
"the whirling wheels."

Each of the cherubim had four faces:
One face was that of a *cherub,*
the second the face of a *man,*
the third the face of a *lion,*
and the fourth the face of an *eagle.*

Then the **cherubim** rose upward.
These were the **living creatures**
I had seen by the Kebar River.

When the *cherubim* moved,
the wheels beside them moved;
and when the *cherubim spread their wings*
to rise from the ground,
the *wheels* did not leave their side.

When the *cherubim* stood still,
they also stood still;
and when the *cherubim* rose,
they rose with them,
because the spirit of the living creatures
was in them.

Then the glory of the LORD
departed from over the threshold of the temple
and stopped above the *cherubim.*

While I watched,
the cherubim spread their wings
and rose from the ground,
and as they went,
the *wheels* went with them.

They stopped at the entrance
to the east gate of the LORD's house,
and the glory of the God of Israel was above them.

These were the **living creatures**
I had seen beneath the **God of Israel** by the Kebar River,
and I realized that they were **cherubim.**

Each had four faces and four wings,
and under their wings
was what looked like the hands of a man.

Their faces had the same appearance
as those I had seen by the Kebar River.
Each one went straight ahead.

Ezekiel 10:1-22

Here I Am, Send Me

I saw the Lord seated on a throne, high and exalted,
and the train of his robe filled the temple.
Above him were seraphs, each with six wings:
With two wings they covered their faces,
with two they covered their feet, and with two they were flying.
And they were calling to one another:
"Holy, holy, holy is the LORD Almighty;
the whole earth is full of his glory."

At the sound of their voices the doorposts and thresholds shook
and the temple was filled with **smoke.**

"Woe to me!" I cried. "I am ruined!
For I am a man of unclean lips,
and I live among a people of unclean lips,
and my eyes have seen the King, the LORD Almighty."

Then one of the seraphs flew to me
with a live coal in his hand,
which he had taken with tongs from the altar.
With it he touched my mouth and said,
"See, this has touched your lips;
your guilt is taken away and your sin atoned for."

Then I heard the voice of the **Lord** saying,
"Whom shall I send? And who will go for us?"
And I said, "Here am I. Send me!"

Isaiah 6:1-8

THE ANCIENT OF DAYS

"As I looked,
**thrones were set in place,
and the Ancient of Days took his seat.**

"His **clothing** was as white as snow;
the **hair** of his head was white like wool.
His **throne** *was flaming with fire, and its* **wheels** *were all ablaze.*

*"A river of fire was flowing, coming out from before him.
Thousands upon thousands attended him;
ten thousand times ten thousand stood before him.
The court was seated, and the books were opened.*

"In my vision at night I looked,
**and there before me was one like a son of man,
coming with the clouds of heaven.**

"He approached the Ancient of Days
and was led into his presence.
He was given
**authority, glory and sovereign power;
all peoples, nations and men of every language
worshiped him.**
*His dominion is an everlasting dominion
that will not pass away,*
and his kingdom is one
that will never be destroyed.

"But the saints of the Most High
will receive the kingdom and will possess it forever—yes,
for ever and ever.

"As I watched,
this little horn was waging war against the saints—
and defeating them,

"until the Ancient of Days came and pronounced judgment
in favor of the saints of the Most High,
and the time came when they possessed the kingdom.

"Another king will arise, different from the earlier ones . . .
He will speak against the Most High and oppress his saints
and try to change the set times and the laws.
The saints will be handed over to him
for a time, times and half a time.

" *'But the court will sit,*
and his power will be taken away
and completely destroyed forever.

" *'Then the sovereignty, power and greatness*
of the kingdoms under the whole heaven
will be handed over to the saints,
the people of the Most High.

" 'His kingdom will be an everlasting kingdom,
and all rulers will worship and obey him.' "

Daniel 7:9-10,13-14,18,21-22,24-27

THE HEAVENLY MAN IN LINEN

In the third year of Cyrus king of Persia, a revelation was given to Daniel. . . . Its message was true and it concerned a great war. The understanding of the message came to him in a vision.

At that time I, Daniel, mourned for three weeks. I ate no choice food; no meat or wine touched my lips; and I used no lotions at all until the three weeks were over. . . . as I was standing on the bank of the great river, the Tigris,

I looked up and there before me was a man dressed in linen,
with a belt of the finest gold around his waist.
His body was like chrysolite,
his face like lightning,
his eyes like flaming torches,
his arms and legs like the gleam of burnished bronze,
and his voice like the sound of a multitude.

I, _____ , was the only one who saw the vision; the men with me did not see it, but such terror overwhelmed them that they fled and hid themselves. So I was left alone, gazing at this great vision; I had no strength left, my face turned deathly pale and I was helpless.

Then I heard him speaking, and as I listened to him,
I fell into a deep sleep, my face to the ground.
A hand touched me
and set me trembling on my hands and knees.

He said, "_____, *you who are highly esteemed,*
consider carefully the words I am about to speak to you,
and stand up, for I have now been sent to you."

And when he said this to me, I stood up trembling.

Then he continued, *"Do not be afraid, _____.*
Since the first day that you set your mind
to gain understanding and to humble yourself
before your God, your words were heard,
and I have come in response to them.

"But **the prince** of the Persian kingdom
resisted me twenty-one days.
Then Michael, one of **the chief princes,** came to help me,
because I was detained there with the **king of Persia.**

"Now I have come to explain to you
what will happen to your people in the future,
for the vision concerns a time yet to come."

While he was saying this to me,
I bowed with my face toward the ground and was speechless.

Then **one who looked like a man** touched my lips,
and I opened my mouth and began to speak.
I said to the one standing before me,
"I am overcome with anguish because of the vision,
my Lord, and I am helpless.
How can I, your servant, talk with you, my lord?
My strength is gone and I can hardly breathe."

Again *the one who looked like a man* touched me
and gave me strength.
"Do not be afraid, O man highly esteemed," he said.
"Peace! Be strong now; be strong."

When he spoke to me, I was strengthened and said,
"Speak, my lord, since you have given me strength."

So he said, *"Do you know why I have come to you?*
Soon I will return to fight against the prince of Persia,
and when I go, the prince of Greece will come;
but first I will tell you what is written in the Book of Truth."

*(No one supports me against them except **Michael,** your **prince.***
And in the first year of Darius the Mede,
I took my stand to support and protect him.)

I heard, but I did not understand. So I asked,
"My lord, what will the outcome of all this be?"

He replied, *"Go your way, Daniel,*
because the words are closed up and sealed
until the time of the end.

"Many will be purified, made spotless and refined,
but the wicked will continue to be wicked.
None of the wicked will understand,
but those who are wise will understand."

Daniel 10:1—11:1; 12:8-10

THE GLORIFIED SON OF MAN

I, John,
your brother and companion
in the **suffering**
and **kingdom**
and **patient endurance**
that are ours in Jesus,
was on the island of Patmos because of the word of God
and the testimony of Jesus.

On the Lord's Day I was in the Spirit,
and I heard behind me a loud voice like a trumpet,
which said:

*"Write on a scroll what you see
and send it to the seven churches. . . . "*

I turned around to see the voice that was speaking to me.
And when I turned
I saw seven golden lampstands,
and among the lampstands was someone
"like a son of man,"
dressed in a robe reaching down to his feet
and with a golden sash around his chest.

His head and hair were white like wool,
as white as snow,
and his eyes were like blazing fire.

His feet were like bronze glowing in a furnace,
and his voice was like the sound of rushing waters.

In his right hand he held seven stars,
and out of his mouth came a sharp double-edged sword.
His face was like the sun shining in all its brilliance.

When I saw him,
I fell at his feet as though dead.

Then he placed his right hand on me and said:

"Do not be afraid.
I am the First and the Last.

"I am the Living One;
I was dead,
and behold I am alive for ever and ever!
And I hold the keys of death and Hades."

Revelation 1:9-18

The Heavenly Throne Room

After this I looked,
and there before me was a door standing open in heaven.
And the voice I had first heard speaking to me like a trumpet
said, *"Come up here,*
and I will show you what must take place after this."

At once I was in the Spirit,
and there before me was a throne in heaven
with someone sitting on it.

And the one who sat there
had the appearance of jasper and carnelian.
A rainbow, resembling an emerald, encircled the throne.

Surrounding the throne were twenty-four other thrones,
and seated on them were twenty-four elders.
They were dressed in white
and had crowns of gold on their heads.

From the throne came flashes of lightning,
rumblings and peals of thunder.
Before the throne, seven lamps were blazing.
These are the seven spirits of God.
Also before the throne there was what looked like
a sea of glass, clear as crystal.

In the center, around the throne, were four living creatures,
and they were covered with eyes, in front and in back.

The first living creature was like a lion,
the second was like an ox,
the third had a face like a man,
the fourth was like a flying eagle.

Each of the four living creatures had six wings
and was covered with eyes all around, even under his wings.

Day and night they never stop saying:
"Holy, holy, holy
is the Lord God Almighty,
who was, and is, and is to come."

Whenever the living creatures give
glory, honor and thanks
to him who sits on the throne
and who lives for ever and ever,
the twenty-four elders fall down before him
who sits on the throne,
and worship him who lives for ever and ever.

They lay their crowns before the throne and say:
"You are worthy, our Lord and God,
to receive **glory**
and **honor**
and **power,**
for you created all things,
and by your will they were created and have their being."

Revelation 4:1-11

FAITHFUL AND TRUE

I saw heaven standing open
and there before me was a white horse,
whose rider is called *Faithful* and *True*.
With justice he judges and makes war.

His *eyes* are like *blazing fire,*
and on his *head* are *many crowns.*
He has *a name* written on him
that no one knows *but he himself.*

He is dressed in a *robe* dipped in *blood,*
and his *name* is the *Word of God.*

The *armies of heaven* were following him,
riding *on white horses and dressed in fine linen,*
white and clean.

Out of his *mouth* comes a *sharp sword*
with which to strike down the nations.
"He will rule them with an iron scepter."
He treads the winepress of the fury of the wrath of
God Almighty.

On his *robe* and on his *thigh*
he has this name written:
KING OF KINGS AND LORD OF LORDS.

Revelation 19:11-16

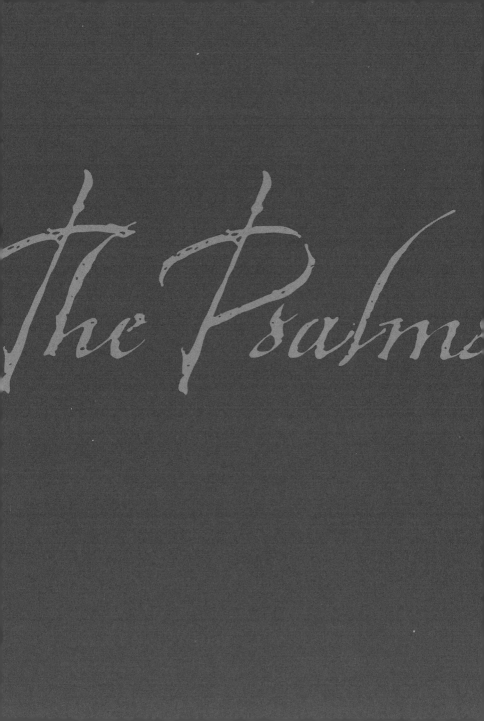

THE PSALMS

I call to God, and the Lord saves me.
Evening, morning and noon I cry out in distress.
and he hears my voice.

INTRODUCTION

Just as the "Prayers of the Prophets" reveal the feelings of God in His pursuit of man, so the psalms reveal the feelings of man in his pursuit of God. And David, author of the majority of the book of Psalms, was an amazing man. He lived in a day when there was no Bible to speak of. Of course, he would have had the first five books of Moses—Genesis, Exodus, Leviticus, Numbers and Deuteronomy—but that would have been about it. The books of Joshua and Judges would have existed in fragments and perhaps other writings called "the Book of the Wars of the LORD" (Num. 21:14). But beyond that, faith in the One true God came out of an individual or corporate experience with Him. David's experiences—his battles, hardships and delights in God—became his own salvation history, a salvation history that impacts all mankind. It is incredible to think that although the psalms were written 3,000 years ago, David's pleasures and struggles with God and his fellow man still have relevance to the situations we face today. In fact, David's relationship with God becomes for us, through the Psalms, an example of how we can relate to God today.

David talked to God a lot. And what did he talk about? His feelings! He brought God into his boring job in the sheep fields and envisioned God as being the Chief Shepherd (see Ps. 23). He told Him how he felt about his enemies (see Ps. 94). He expressed his passionate love for God in unabashed worship (see Ps. 27) and his remorse over his wicked heart in deep repentance (see Ps. 51). He took all his feelings to God. Written from the perspective of a relatively uncultured tribesman, who eked out an existence living off the land, David writes amazingly some of the loftiest, spiritual prose known to man. The inspiration for David's psalms came from several sources: (1) reflection on God's work in nature and history; (2) direct revelation and unction (see 1 Chron. 28:11-12,19); and (3) the way God worked in his life. We can imagine the scene as God inspired David in the dim, spiritually charged atmosphere of the Tabernacle where many of these psalms may have been composed and recorded on-site—faithful scribes sitting in the corner, quill and leather page in hand, ready to capture David's spontaneous "Songs to the Lord." Later David's books of praise and worship were collected and patched together with the works of other psalmists to become the first musical prayer book of God's people.

Inspired by God, David set up an elaborate system of worship, praise and prayer that became the pattern ever after (see 1 Chron. 23:27-28,30; 25:1). In summary, the entire system was "prescribed by David and Gad the king's seer and Nathan the prophet; this was commanded by the LORD through his prophets" (2 Chron. 29:25). Later, whenever the fallen nation came back to God and reopened the Temple, the prescribed worship was put back into place "as prescribed by David" (Ezra 3:10; Neh. 12:24). This is the recurring pattern in all the Old Testament revivals. Each time there was repentance, the leaders commanded all the people of God to pray the psalms, such as Jehoshaphat circa 900 B.C. (see

2 Chron. 20), Hezekiah circa 726-725 B.C. (see 2 Chron. 29—30), Josiah circa 625-623 B.C. (see 2 Chron. 35) and Ezra and Nehemiah circa 450 B.C. (see Ezra 3:10-13; Neh. 12:24).

Thus it was that God used the passionate emotions of David's heart to give expression to what He was searching for in true worship. David was a worshiper and intercessor, par excellence. It was said of him that he was "a man after my [God's] own heart" (Acts 13:22). His passion for God was so extraordinary that one might say Israel's elaborate system of worship, dance and praise grew out of this one man's devotion. What David did has never been forgotten by God. And we get to say his prayers. We get to enter his worship through his words. And what are his words about? A simplistic view could break them down into three or four categories. First, the "I love you, I love you, I love you" psalms of worship and devotion. Second, the "I love you and I'm sorry I blew it" psalms of repentance. And finally, the "I love you, but I'm in trouble—Help" psalms. If we wanted to consider a fourth, it would be the "Help! Now get 'em God" imprecatory psalms.

Examining these categories in greater detail, 1 Chronicles 16:4 says, "He [David] appointed some of the Levites to minister before the ark of the LORD, to make petition, to give thanks, and to praise the LORD, the God of Israel." David uses various nuances to describe the larger, "I love you, I love you, I love you" dimension of prayer. In this one verse, the four verbs are:

- to minister, *sharath*, meaning "to attend, serve, or wait on";
- to make petition, *zakar*, which means "to be mindful by recounting and recording, and then causing what is remembered to be continually thought upon";

- to give thanks, *yadah*, literally meaning "to hold out the hand, to throw or shoot at or away"; hence, it came to be associated with worship as the extending or throwing up of the hands, to confess or exalt with thanks; and
- to praise the Lord, *halal*, from which we get "hallelujah."

Originally, "praise," or "halal," came from a primitive root word that meant "to be clear of sound, or more usually of color." It eventually metamorphosed into "to shine"; whereafter, the word came to be associated with worship and took on the idea of praising God with outrageous celebration. This is how David prescribed worshipers to minister to God. Davidic worship, then, is glorious praise in celebration and devotion.

The second category is the "I love you and I'm sorry I blew it" repentance psalms. They teach us how to say "I'm sorry," and, contrary to popular opinion, love does mean having to say you're sorry. Many people need language to articulate the repentance in their hearts. Children also need to learn how to say they're sorry. Since we live in a fallen world, repentance, forgiveness and acceptance are necessary many times throughout our lives. These psalms help us to know both how to ask for and receive forgiveness.

Thirdly, the "I love you, but I'm in trouble—Help" psalms are prayers for people in crisis. Life is filled with crises, both big and small. David was never too proud to ask for help when he needed it, no matter if he had been good or bad. And he always knew that God would listen and be there for him in all of his many trials. Sometimes he added a thought to these prayers, namely, "as you get me out of here, get them too!" He gives expression to feelings we all have but feel guilty articulating.

David prayed such things boldly, because he knew his heart was for God; therefore, God was on his side. He was asking for justice, and he wasn't afraid to pray for it. Although we don't want impure judgments to come back on us, there is a place to "judge righteous judgment" (John 7:24, *KJV*). And the psalms of David show us how to do this.

By the New Testament era, the psalms were considered the most important of Old Testament books. *The International Standard Bible Encyclopaedia* says,

> There has never been any serious question as to the right of the Psalter to a place in the Canon of Scripture. The book is possibly more highly esteemed among Christians than by the Jews. If Christians were permitted to retain only one book in the Old Testament, they would almost certainly choose the Psalms.[1]

The New Testament states that if you are filled with the Holy Spirit, then praying the psalms will be a natural outcome (see Eph. 5:17-20). All followers of God prayed the psalms (see Acts 2:42; Col. 3:16; Jas. 5:13), and the Church has continued this practice for 2,000 years. From the Early Church on, all monks and nuns prayed the whole book of psalms every week. St. Patrick, the famous missionary evangelist to Ireland, was said to recite at least 100 psalms a day out loud to God. Following his example, the Celtic spiritual iron-men began to pray "the three fifties" daily, that is, the entire book of Psalms every day. You, too, can continue this great tradition by beginning to pray the psalms every day. When they connect with your heart, you will worship as David did. And God will be blessed.

BLESSED IS THE MAN

Blessed is the man
who does not walk in the counsel of the wicked
or stand in the way of sinners
or sit in the seat of mockers.

But his delight is in the law of the LORD,
and on his law he meditates
day and night.

He is like a tree planted by streams of water,
which yields its fruit in season
and whose leaf does not wither.

Whatever he does prospers.

Not so the wicked!

They are like chaff that the wind blows away.
Therefore the wicked will not stand in the judgment,
nor sinners in the assembly of the righteous.

For the LORD
watches over the way of the righteous,
but the way of the wicked will perish.

Psalm 1:1-6

FEARFULLY AND WONDERFULLY MADE

O LORD,
you have searched me and you know me.

You know when I sit and when I rise;
you perceive my thoughts from afar.
You discern my going out and my lying down;
you are familiar with all my ways.

Before a word is on my tongue
you know it completely, *O LORD.*
You hem me in—behind and before;
you have laid your hand upon me.

Such knowledge is too wonderful for me,
too lofty for me to attain.

Where can I go from your Spirit?
Where can I flee from your presence?
If I go up to the heavens,
you are there;
if I make my bed in the depths,
you are there.

If I rise on the wings of the dawn,
if I settle on the far side of the sea,
even there your hand will guide me,
your right hand will hold me fast.

If I say, "Surely the darkness will hide me
and the light become night around me,"
even the darkness will not be dark to you;
the night will shine like the day,
for darkness is as light to you.

For you created my inmost being;
you knit me together in my mother's womb.

I praise you because I am fearfully and wonderfully made;
your works are wonderful, I know that full well.

My frame was not hidden from you
when I was made in the secret place.
When I was woven together in the depths of the earth,
Your eyes saw my unformed body.

All the days ordained for me
were written in your book
before one of them came to be.

How precious to me are your thoughts, O God!
How vast is the sum of them!
Were I to count them,
they would outnumber the grains of sand.
When I awake, I am still with you.

If only you would slay the wicked, O God!
Away from me, you bloodthirsty men!
They speak of you with evil intent;
your adversaries misuse your name.

Do I not hate those who hate you, O LORD,
and abhor those who rise up against you?
I have nothing but hatred for them;
I count them my enemies.

Search me, O God,
and know my heart;
test me and know my anxious thoughts.
See if there is any offensive way in me,
and lead me in the way everlasting.

Psalm 139:1-24

A Prayer of Repentance

Have mercy on me, O God,
according to your unfailing love;
according to your great compassion blot out my transgressions.
Wash away all my iniquity and cleanse me from my sin.

For I know my transgressions,
and my sin is always before me.

Against you, you only,
have I sinned and done what is evil in your sight,
so that you are proved right when you speak
and justified when you judge.

Surely I was sinful at birth,
sinful from the time my mother conceived me.
Surely you desire truth in the inner parts;
you teach me wisdom in the inmost place.

Cleanse me with hyssop, and I will be clean;
wash me, and I will be whiter than snow.
Let me hear joy and gladness;
let the bones you have crushed rejoice.

Hide your face from my sins
and blot out all my iniquity.

Create in me a pure heart, O God,
and renew a steadfast spirit within me.
Do not cast me from your presence
or take your Holy Spirit from me.

Restore to me the joy of your salvation
and grant me a willing spirit, to sustain me.
Then I will teach transgressors your ways,
and sinners will turn back to you.

Save me from bloodguilt, O God,
the God who saves me,
and my tongue will sing of your righteousness.

O Lord, open my lips,
and my mouth will declare your praise.

You do not delight in sacrifice,
or I would bring it;
you do not take pleasure in offerings.

The sacrifices of God are a broken spirit;
a broken and contrite heart,
O God, you will not despise.

In your good pleasure make *Zion* prosper;
make the *Church* prosper;
build up the walls of *Jerusalem.*

Then there will be *righteous sacrifices,*
and *offerings* to delight you;
then *true worship* will be offered on your altar.

Psalm 51:1-19

SAVE ME, O GOD

Keep me safe, O God, for in you I take refuge.
I said to the LORD,
"You are my Lord; apart from you I have no good thing."
As for the saints who are in the land,
they are the glorious ones in whom is all my delight.
The sorrows of those will increase who run after other gods.
I will not pour out their libations of blood
or take up their names on my lips.

LORD, you have assigned me my portion and my cup;
you have made my lot secure.
The boundary lines have fallen for me in pleasant places;
surely I have a delightful inheritance.
I will praise the LORD, who counsels me;
even at night my heart instructs me.

I have set the LORD always before me.
Because he is at my right hand, I will not be shaken.

Therefore my heart is glad and my tongue rejoices;
my body also will rest secure,
because you will not abandon me to the grave,
nor will you let your Holy One see decay.

You have made known to me the path of life;
you will fill me with joy in your presence,
with eternal pleasures at your right hand.

Psalm 16:1-11

THE LORD IS MY SHEPHERD

The LORD is my shepherd,
I shall not be in want.
He makes me lie down in *green pastures,*
he leads me beside *quiet waters,*
he restores my soul.

He guides me in paths of righteousness
for his name's sake.

Even though I walk through the valley
of the shadow of death,
I will fear no evil,
for you are with me;
your rod and your staff,
they comfort me.

You *prepare a table* before me
in the presence of my enemies.
You anoint my head with oil;
my cup overflows.

Surely goodness and love
will follow me all the days of my life,
and I will dwell in the house of the LORD
forever.

Psalm 23

BATTLE HYMN OF THE KING

I love You, **O LORD,** my strength.
The **LORD** is my **rock,** my **fortress** and my **deliverer;**
my God is my **rock,** in whom I take **refuge.**
He is my **shield** and the **horn** of my salvation, my **stronghold.**
I call to the LORD, who is worthy of praise,
and I am saved from my enemies.

The cords of **death** entangled me;
the torrents of **destruction** overwhelmed me.
The cords of the **grave** coiled around me;
the snares of **death** confronted me.

In my distress **I called** to the LORD;
I cried to my God for help.
From his temple **he heard** my voice;
my cry came before him, into his ears.

The earth trembled and quaked,
and the foundations of the mountains shook;
they trembled because he was angry.

Smoke rose from his nostrils;
consuming fire came from his mouth,
burning coals blazed out of it.
He **parted the heavens and came down;**
dark clouds were under his feet.
He **mounted the cherubim** and flew;
he **soared** on the wings of the wind.

He made **darkness** his **covering,**
his canopy around him—the **dark rain clouds** of the sky.
Out of the **brightness** *of his presence* **clouds** *advanced,*
with **hailstones** and **bolts of lightning.**

The LORD **thundered** from heaven;
the **voice** of the **Most High** resounded.
He shot his **arrows** *and scattered the enemies,*
great **bolts of lightning** and routed them.

He reached down from on high and **took hold of me;**
he **drew me out** of deep waters.
He **rescued me** from my powerful enemy,
from my foes, who were too strong for me.

They confronted me in the day of my disaster,
but the LORD was my support.
He brought me out into a spacious place;
he rescued me because he delighted in me.

The LORD has dealt with me according to my righteousness;
according to the cleanness of my hands he has rewarded me.

For I have kept the ways of the LORD;
I have not done evil by turning from my God.
All his laws are before me;
I have not turned away from his decrees.
I have been blameless before him
and have kept myself from sin.

The LORD has rewarded me according to my righteousness,
according to the cleanness of my hands in his sight.

To the *faithful* you show yourself *faithful,*
to the *blameless* you show yourself *blameless,*
to the *pure* you show yourself *pure,*
but to the *crooked* you show yourself *shrewd.*
You save the *humble*
but bring low those whose eyes are *haughty.*

You, O LORD, keep my lamp burning;
my God turns my darkness into light.
With your help I can advance against a troop;
with my God I can scale a wall.

For who is God besides the LORD?
And who is the Rock except our God?
It is God who *arms me with strength*
and makes my way perfect.

He *makes my feet* like the feet of a *deer;*
he enables me to *stand on the heights.*
He *trains my hands* for battle;
my arms can bend a bow of bronze.

You give me your shield of victory,
and your right hand sustains me;
you stoop down to make me great.
You broaden the path beneath me,
so that my ankles do not turn.

I pursued my enemies and overtook them;
I did not turn back till they were destroyed.
I crushed them so that they could not rise;
they fell beneath my feet.

You armed me with strength for battle;
you made my adversaries bow at my feet.
You made my enemies turn their backs in flight,
and I destroyed my foes.

They cried for help, but there was no one to save them—
to the LORD, but he did not answer.
I beat them as fine as dust borne on the wind;
I poured them out like mud in the streets.

. . . You have made me the head of nations;
people I did not know are subject to me.

The LORD lives!
Praise be to my Rock!
Exalted be God my Savior!

Therefore I will praise you among the nations,
O LORD;
I will sing praises to your name.

He gives his king great victories;
he shows unfailing kindness to his anointed,
to David and his descendants forever.

Psalm 18:1-14,16-29,31-43,46,49-50

UNDER THE SHADOW OF HIS WINGS

He who dwells in the shelter of the Most High
will rest in the shadow of the Almighty.

I will say of the LORD,
"He is my refuge and my fortress,
my God, in whom I trust."

Surely he will save you from the fowler's snare
and from the deadly pestilence.

He will cover you with his feathers,
and under his wings you will find refuge;
his faithfulness will be your shield and rampart.

You will not fear the terror of night,
nor the arrow that flies by day,
nor the pestilence that stalks in the darkness,
nor the plague that destroys at midday.

A thousand may fall at your side,
ten thousand at your right hand,
but it will not come near you.

You will only observe with your eyes
and see the punishment of the wicked.

If you make the Most High your dwelling—
even the LORD, who is my refuge—
then no harm will befall you,
no disaster will come near your tent.

For he will command his angels concerning you
to guard you in all your ways;
they will lift you up in their hands,
so that you will not strike your foot against a stone.

You will tread upon the lion and the cobra;
you will trample the great lion and the serpent.

"Because he loves me," says the LORD,
"I will rescue him;
I will protect him,
for he acknowledges my name.

"He will call upon me,
and I will answer him;
I will be with him in trouble,
I will deliver him and honor him.

"With long life will I satisfy him
and show him my salvation."

Psalm 91

BETTER IS ONE DAY

How lovely is your dwelling place,
O LORD Almighty!

My soul yearns, even faints,
for the courts of the LORD;
my heart and my flesh cry out
for the living God.

Even the sparrow has found a home,
and the swallow a nest for herself,
where she may have her young—
a place near your altar,
O LORD Almighty,
my King and my God.

Blessed are those who dwell in your house;
they are ever praising you.
Selah

Blessed are those whose strength is in you,
who have set their hearts on pilgrimage.

As they pass through the Valley of Baca,
they make it a place of springs;
the autumn rains also cover it with pools.

They go from strength to strength,
till each appears before God in Zion.

Hear my prayer,
O LORD God Almighty;
listen to me, O God of Jacob.
Selah

Look upon our shield, O God;
look with favor on your anointed one.

Better is one day in your courts
than a thousand elsewhere;

I would rather be a doorkeeper
in the house of my God
than dwell in the tents of the wicked.

For the LORD God is a sun and shield;
the LORD bestows favor and honor;
no good thing does he withhold
from those whose walk is blameless.

O LORD Almighty,
blessed is the man who trusts in you.

Psalm 84

Jesus' Prayer from the Cross

My God, my God,
why have you forsaken me?
Why are you so far from saving me,
so far from the words of my groaning?

O my God, I cry out by day, but you do not answer,
by night, and am not silent.
Yet you are enthroned as the Holy One;
you are the praise of Israel.
In you our fathers put their trust;
they trusted and you delivered them.
They cried to you and were saved;
in you they trusted and were not disappointed.

But I am a worm and not a man,
scorned by men and despised by the people.
All who see me mock me;
they hurl insults, shaking their heads:

"He trusts in the LORD; let the LORD rescue him.
Let him deliver him, since he delights in him."

Yet you brought me out of the womb;
you made me trust in you even at my mother's breast.
From birth I was cast upon you;
from my mother's womb you have been my God.

Do not be far from me,
for trouble is near and there is no one to help.

Many bulls surround me; strong bulls of Bashan encircle me.
Roaring lions tearing their prey
open their mouths wide against me.

I am poured out like water, and all my bones are out of joint.
My heart has turned to wax; it has melted away within me.
My strength is dried up like [clay] . . .
and my tongue sticks to the roof of my mouth;
you lay me in the dust of death.

Dogs have surrounded me;
a band of evil men has encircled me,
they have pierced my hands and my feet.
I can count all my bones; people stare and gloat over me.
They divide my garments among them
and cast lots for my clothing.

But you, O LORD, be not far off;
O my Strength, come quickly to help me.
Deliver my life from the sword,
my precious life from the power of the dogs.
Rescue me from the mouth of the lions;
save me from the horns of the wild oxen.

I will declare your name to my brothers;
in the congregation I will praise You.

You who fear the LORD, praise him!
All you descendants of Jacob, honor him!
Revere him, all you descendants of Israel!

For he has not despised or disdained
the suffering of the afflicted one;
he has not hidden his face from him
but has listened to his cry for help.

From you comes the theme of my praise in the great assembly;
before those who fear you will I fulfill my vows.
The poor will eat and be satisfied;
they who seek the LORD will praise him—
may your hearts live forever!

All the ends of the earth will remember
and turn to the LORD,
and all the families of the nations
will bow down before him,
for dominion belongs to the LORD
and he rules over the nations.

All the rich of the earth will feast and worship;
all who go down to the dust will kneel before him—
those who cannot keep themselves alive.

Posterity will serve him;
future generations will be told about the Lord.

They will proclaim his righteousness
to a people yet unborn—[Why?]
For he has done it!

Psalm 22

LIFT UP YOUR HEADS

The earth is the LORD's, and everything in it,
the world, and all who live in it;
for he founded it upon the seas and established it upon the waters.

Who may ascend the hill of the LORD?
Who may stand in his holy place?
He who has clean hands and a pure heart,
who does not lift up his soul to an idol
or swear by what is false.
He will receive blessing from the LORD
and vindication from God his Savior.
Such is the generation of those who seek him,
who seek your face, O God of Jacob.

Lift up your heads, O you gates;
be lifted up, you ancient doors,
that the King of glory may come in.

Who is this King of glory?
The LORD strong and mighty, the LORD mighty in battle.

Lift up your heads, O you gates;
lift them up, you ancient doors,
that the King of glory may come in.

Who is he, this King of glory?
The LORD Almighty—he is the King of glory.

Psalm 24

A Prayer for Leaders

May the LORD *answer you* when you are in distress;
may the name of the God of Jacob *protect you.*

May he send *you help* from the sanctuary
and grant *you support* from Zion.
May he *remember* all your sacrifices
and *accept* your burnt offerings.
Selah

May he give you the desire of your heart
and make all your plans succeed.
We will *shout for joy* when you are victorious
and will *lift up our banners* in the name of our God.

May the LORD grant all your requests.

Now I know that the LORD *saves his anointed*;
he *answers him* from his holy heaven
with the *saving power* of his right hand.

Some trust in chariots and some in horses,
but we trust in the name of the LORD our God.
They are brought to their knees and fall,
but we rise up and stand firm.

O Lord, save the king!
Answer us when we call!

Psalm 20

A Blessing Psalm of Ascents

Blessed are all who fear the LORD,
who walk in his ways.

You will eat the fruit of your labor;
blessings and prosperity will be yours.

Your wife
will be like a fruitful vine within your house;
your sons
will be like olive shoots around your table.

Thus is the man blessed who fears the LORD.

May the LORD bless you from Zion
all the days of your life;

may you see the prosperity of Jerusalem,
and may you live to see your children's children.

Peace be upon Israel.

[Peace be upon the Church.]

Psalm 128

PRAYERS OF WISDOM

Wisdom calls aloud in the street.
She raises her voice in the public squares.

INTRODUCTION

In ancient times, wisdom literature was a common means of helping one live life. Hebrew wisdom literature from Proverbs, Ecclesiastes and Job is some of the most highly acclaimed literature in this particular genre and remains today the most widely read writing of its kind. As wisdom literature, its popularity is unrivaled. The sheer brilliance of its work points to supernatural authorship. To this day, its practical applications to all facets of life render it a favorite with businessmen, motivational speakers, leaders, parents and educators of all types. In fact, the wisdom contained in these small books lies at the root of modern Western civilization, the English-speaking world in particular. For instance, in early America, the book of Proverbs was taught to children in schools across the country in order to instill in them a strong work ethic and a basis for morality. Even today, principled men and women apply this same wisdom to their daily lives and are successful because of it. Simply put, praying prayers of wisdom will help you live life well, for it was for this purpose that they were written.

The aim of prayers of wisdom is laid out in Proverbs 1:1-4:

The Proverbs of Solomon son of David, king of Israel:
for attaining wisdom and discipline; for understanding

words of insight; for acquiring a disciplined and prudent life, doing what is right and just and fair; for giving prudence to the simple, knowledge and discretion to the young—

Here you see that wisdom is understood as the proper application of spirituality to daily life. Once you have had your head in the heavenlies, praying the theophanies, with its clouds, thunders and visions of the throne room, how do you walk when your feet hit the ground? The answers found in prayers of wisdom are simple: Among other things, don't be lazy, do not tarry long at the wine, love your wife and remember God in all that you do. These are the things that will make you a wise son and a good father, or a wholesome daughter and a noble wife.

In *The Book of Prayers*, the prayers of wisdom have been arranged topically and deal with ordinary subjects such as wisdom, work, speech, sex and adultery, mercy, virtue, leadership, relationships and spirituality. These prayers connect with the concerns that all of us have. Who among us could not use divine help with these things here on Earth? By applying the wisdom found in these prayers, we avoid the many pitfalls of life, thereby saving ourselves from much distress.

I happened to stumble upon the book of Proverbs during one of the most confusing times of my life. I was in university and having a difficult time reconciling my relatively new faith with all that I was being taught in class. Often I found myself full of doubt, bewildered by all the data coming at me. It was at this point in my life that I discovered the prayers of wisdom. A preacher had said that there was a chapter of the book of Proverbs for every day of the month and that it would be wise to read one a day. Armed with this new piece of advice, I launched out and began to read them in my customary fashion—praying each proverb slowly, word by word. As I faithfully prayed through them day after day, the wisdom theme stuck out. I became intrigued with the whole concept. Wisdom is, the Bible says, more profitable than silver, gold or rubies; nothing I could desire compares with her (see Prov. 3:13-15).

This thought set me on a quest for wisdom. I combed the Scriptures for every reference I could find. In the end, I came back to where I started and found that, "The fear of the LORD is the beginning of wisdom, and knowledge of the Holy One is understanding" (Prov. 9:10). I continued to pray the proverbs every day for months on end, and eventually came out of my confusion. By the end of my time at university, in certain ways I was "wiser than my enemies . . . I [had] more insight than all my teachers, for I meditate[d] on your statutes" (Ps. 119:98-99). Praying prayers of wisdom will make a tangible difference in our daily lives.

We recommend praying all the prayers of wisdom found in this section. Children and teenagers, especially, should be praying for this divine wisdom daily, since they are growing up in a culture increasingly contrary to these wise ways. Your daily life will improve significantly if you pray them repeatedly until they are impressed upon your heart.

A Time for Everything

**There is a time for everything,
and a season for every activity under heaven:**

*a time to be **born** and a time to **die**,
a time to **plant** and a time to **uproot**,
a time to **kill** and a time to **heal**,
a time to **tear down** and a time to **build**,
a time to **weep** and a time to **laugh**,
a time to **mourn** and a time to **dance**,
a time to **scatter stones** and a time to **gather them**,
a time to **embrace** and a time to **refrain**,
a time to **search** and a time to **give up**,
a time to **keep** and a time to **throw away**,
a time to **tear** and a time to **mend**,
a time to be **silent** and a time to **speak**,
a time to **love** and a time to **hate**,
a time for **war** and a time for **peace**.*

*He has made everything beautiful in its time.
He has also set eternity in the hearts of men;*
yet they cannot fathom what God has done
from beginning to end.

Ecclesiastes 3:1-8,11

Wisdom Calls Out

LORD, *you have said:*
My son, if you accept my words
and store up my commands within you,
turning your ear to wisdom
and applying your heart to understanding,
and if you call out for insight
and cry aloud for understanding,
and if you look for it as for silver
and search for it as for hidden treasure,
then you will understand the fear of the LORD
and find the knowledge of God.
For the LORD gives wisdom,
and from his mouth come knowledge and understanding.

Father, I ask for this heart of wisdom, and I believe:
The fear of the LORD is the beginning of wisdom,
and knowledge of the Holy One is understanding.
For through me your days will be many,
and years will be added to your life.

So I say to wisdom, "You are my sister,"
and I call understanding "my kinsman."
I will apply my heart to instruction
and my ears to words of knowledge.

Wisdom is supreme; therefore, I will get wisdom.
Though it cost me all I have, I will get understanding.

Proverbs 2:1-6; 9:10-11; 7:4; 23:12; 4:7

THE RIGHTEOUS WORKMAN

I went past the field of the sluggard,
past the vineyard of the man who lacks judgment;
thorns had come up everywhere, weeds covered the ground.
I applied my heart to what I observed and learned a lesson
from what I saw: A little sleep, a little slumber,
a little folding of the hands to rest—and poverty
will come on you like a bandit and scarcity like an armed man.

LORD, you have said:
that I am not to wear myself out to get rich;
but to have the wisdom to show restraint.
Yet, you have also said, all hard work brings a profit,
but mere talk leads only to poverty.

I ask you to help me be a wise son.
For lazy hands make a man poor,
but diligent hands bring wealth.
He who gathers crops in summer is a wise son,
but he who sleeps during harvest is a disgraceful son.
Deliver me from the sins and excuses of the sluggard who says,
"There is a lion in the road, a fierce lion roaming the streets!"
As a door turns on its hinges, I'll just turn on my bed.

For the one who is slack in his work
is brother to him that is a great waster.
As you have said, show me a man skilled in his work;
he will serve before kings, not before obscure men.

Proverbs 24:30-34; 23:4; 14:23; 10:4-5; 26:13-14; 18:9; 22:29

LET MY WORDS BE FEW

" . . . I will watch my ways and keep my tongue from sin;
I will put a muzzle on my mouth
as long as the wicked are in my presence."

Father, help me to guard my lips, because
he who guards his lips guards his life,
but he who speaks rashly will come to ruin.
For life and death are in the power of the tongue,
and reckless words pierce like a sword,
but the tongue of the wise brings healing.
When words are many, sin is not absent,
but he who holds his tongue is wise.

Give me the gentle answer that turns away wrath,
instead of a harsh word that stirs up anger.
For it is to a man's honor to avoid strife,
but every fool is quick to quarrel.
A fool shows his annoyance at once,
but a prudent man overlooks an insult.

LORD, grow the fruit of self-control in my life,
for through patience even a ruler can be persuaded,
and a gentle tongue can break a bone.
I will not be quick with my mouth,
for you, O God, are in heaven, and I am on earth,
so I will let my words be few.

Psalm 39:1; Proverbs 13:3; 18:21; 12:18; 10:19; 15:1; 20:3; 12:16;
25:15; Ecclesiastes 5:2

DELIVER ME FROM EVIL

"I made a covenant with my eyes
not to look lustfully at a girl."
For you, O LORD, see my ways and count my every step.
Father, I ask that you keep me from the immoral woman,
from the smooth tongue of the wayward wife.
Do not let me lust in my heart after her beauty
or let her captivate me with her eyes,
for the prostitute reduces a man to a loaf of bread,
and the adulteress preys upon your very life.
Can a man take fire into his lap without being burned?
So is he who sleeps with another man's wife;
no one who touches her will go unpunished.
"This is the way of an adulteress: She eats
and wipes her mouth and says, 'I've done nothing wrong.'"
But you say, a man who commits adultery lacks judgment;
whoever does . . . his shame will never be wiped away.
For her house leads down to death. . . .
None who go to her return or attain the paths of life.

So I will drink water from my own cistern,
running water from my own well.
I will rejoice in the wife of my youth.
As a loving doe, a graceful deer—may her breasts satisfy me
always; let me ever be captivated by her love.
For I know that my ways are in full view of you, O LORD,
and you examine all my paths.

Job 31:1,4; Proverbs 6:24-27,29; 30:20; 6:32-33;
2:18-19; 5:15,18-19,21

MERCY

Father in Heaven, you have said:
He who oppresses the poor shows contempt for their Maker,
but whoever is kind to the needy honors God.
Rich and poor have this in common:
The LORD is the Maker of them all.
So I will not exploit the poor because they are poor
nor crush the needy in court, for you will take up their case
and will plunder those who plunder them.

The righteous care about justice for the poor,
but the wicked have no such concern.
And you say, he who is kind to the poor lends to the LORD,
and he will reward him for what he has done.

Let me be like Job, who said:
I rescued the poor who cried for help,
and the fatherless who had none to assist him.
The man who was dying blessed me;
I made the widow's heart sing.
I was eyes to the blind and feet to the lame.
I was a father to the needy; I took up the case of the stranger.
I broke the fangs of the wicked
and snatched the victims from their teeth.
I chose the way for them and sat as their chief;
I dwelt as a king among his troops;
I was like one who comforts mourners.

Proverbs 14:31; 22:2,22-23; 29:7; 19:17; Job 29:12-13,15-17,25

VIRTUE AND HONOR

Father, my prayer is that I will pay attention to what you say,
and listen closely to your words.
For they are life to those who find them
and health to a man's whole body.
Above all else, I will guard my heart, for it is the wellspring of life.
For he who pursues righteousness and love
finds life, prosperity and honor.

I will put away perversity from my mouth,
and keep corrupt talk far from my lips.
I will make level paths for my feet,
and take only ways that are firm.
For a good name is more desirable than great riches;
to be esteemed is better than silver or gold.

LORD, I will honor you with my wealth,
with the firstfruits of all my crops;
then, as you have said, my barns will be filled to overflowing,
and my vats will brim over with new wine.

Help me to walk with the wise,
for he who walks with the wise grows wise,
but a companion of fools suffers harm.
I will not be misled: ***"Bad company corrupts good character."***
But the fear of the LORD adds length to life,
but the years of the wicked are cut short.

Proverbs 4:20,22-23; 21:21; 4:24,26; 22:1; 3:9-10; 13:20;
1 Corinthians 15:33; Proverbs 10:27

THE WAY OF A KING

There are three things that are stately in their stride,
four that move with stately bearing:
a lion, mighty among beasts, who retreats before nothing;
a strutting rooster, a he-goat, and a *king with his army* . . .

Father, you say that it is the glory of God to conceal a matter,
but to search out a matter is the glory of kings.
So I ask for the wisdom to search out your ways,
for by wisdom kings reign and rulers make laws that are just;
and by it princes govern, and all nobles rule on earth.
For it is better to be a poor but wise youth than
an old but foolish king who no longer takes warning.

I ask for a heart to rule justly;
for by justice a king gives a country stability,
and if a king judges the poor with fairness,
his throne will always be secure.

I pray also for kingly character, for as you say,
"O my son, O son of my womb, O son of my vows,
do not spend your strength on women,
your vigor on those who ruin kings.
It is not for kings, O Lemuel—not for kings to drink wine, not for rulers to
crave beer, lest they drink and forget what the law decrees,
and deprive all the oppressed of their rights.
Speak up for those who cannot speak for themselves,
for the rights of all who are destitute."

Proverbs 30:29-31; 25:2; 8:15-16; Ecclesiastes 4:13;
Proverbs 29:4,14; 31:2-5,8

In Praise of the Noble Wife

A wife of noble character who can find?
She is worth far more than rubies.
Her husband has full confidence in her and lacks nothing of value.
She brings him good, not harm, all the days of her life.
She is like the merchant ships, bringing her food from afar.
She gets up while it is still dark;
she provides food for her family and portions for her servant girls.
She considers a field and buys it;
out of her earnings she plants a vineyard.
She sets about her work vigorously;
her arms are strong for her tasks.
She sees that her trading is profitable,
and her lamp does not go out at night.
She opens her arms to the poor and extends her hands to the needy.

Her husband is respected at the city gate,
where he takes his seat among the elders of the land.
She is clothed with strength and dignity;
she can laugh at the days to come.
She speaks with wisdom, and faithful instruction is on her tongue.
She watches over the affairs of her household
and does not eat the bread of idleness.

Her children arise and call her blessed;
her husband also, and he praises her:
"Many women do noble things, but you surpass them all."
Charm is deceptive, and beauty is fleeting;
but a woman who fears the LORD is to be praised.
Give her the reward she has earned,
and let her works bring her praise at the city gate.

Proverbs 31:10-12,14-18,20,23,25-31

THE WHOLE DUTY OF MAN

[LORD, you have said:]
Remember your Creator in the days of your youth,
before the days of trouble come
and the years approach when you will say,
"I find no pleasure in them"—
before the sun and the light and the moon . . . grow dark,
when the keepers of the house tremble, and the strong men stoop,
when the grinders cease because they are few,
and those looking through the windows grow dim;
when men rise up at the sound of birds,
but all their songs grow faint;
when men are afraid of heights and of dangers in the streets;
and the grasshopper drags himself along
and desire no longer is stirred.
Then man goes to his eternal home
and mourners go about the streets.

Remember him—before the silver cord is severed,
or the golden bowl is broken;
and the dust returns to the ground it came from,
and the spirit returns to God who gave it.

Now all has been heard; here is the conclusion of the matter:
Fear God and keep his commandments,
for this is the whole duty of man.
For God will bring every deed into judgment,
including every hidden thing, whether it is good or evil.

Ecclesiastes 12:1-7,13-14

THE SONG
OF SONGS

Love is as strong as death, its jealousy unyielding as the grave. It burns like blasting fire, like a mighty flame.

INTRODUCTION

It is a big jump to move from praying to Abba Father to praying directly to the Bridegroom. Intimacy with the Father looks very different from intimacy with the Lover. I well remember, many years ago, my first attempt to pray the Song of Songs. I found myself immediately aware that I was in over my head. I was trying to be faithful to the text, but I was embarrassed to be talking to God in such graphic terms. In the end, blushing, I told the Lord that I could not continue unless He helped me figure out what I was even talking about.

Many people meet similar problems in their initial endeavors to pray the Song of Songs. How does one deal with all the sexual imagery? Why is this book even in the Bible? Still more confusing is knowing how to approach this book in prayer. To start with, a distinction must be made between its literal and allegorical interpretations, understanding that it certainly conveys both dimensions to the reader. The historical-literal approach maintains that the relationship described is a real one between Solomon and a poor Shulammite woman, and through it, the purity, beauty and satisfaction of marital love can be seen. The tone is clearly erotic, but it is Eros undefiled. As such, it sets the standard for human love as God Himself created and intended it to be.

The allegorical interpretation, on the other hand, would be that the Song of Songs depicts the figurative relationship between Jehovah/Jesus, as Lover and Bridegroom, and Israel/the Church, as His beloved Bride. This is the approach most often taken by Jews and Christians throughout the ages:

> The favorite image used for portraying the relationship between Jehovah and His chosen people is that of marriage. Jehovah is the Spouse, Israel, the bride, and the Temple is the house where the conjugal relations, always spiritual in nature, take place. This image is fully developed by Hosea and Ezekiel; however, as early as Exodus, Jehovah appears to Israel as a jealous God, and in the books of the prophets, the commission of sin, especially the sin of idolatry, is called infidelity or adultery. In the Gospel, the Kingdom of heaven is on several occasions compared to a wedding feast. St. Paul says he betrothed the Corinthians to the Spouse, Christ, and St. John in the Apocalypse gives us the image of the Lamb with Jerusalem, His bride.[1]

All of this imagery culminates in an Ephesians passage, in which the mystical relationship between Christ and His Church is compared to the physical union of marriage. "For this cause a man shall leave his father and mother, and shall cleave to his wife; and the two shall become one flesh. This mystery is great; but I am speaking with reference to Christ and the church" (Eph. 5:31-32, *NASB*). Here Paul is using marriage as an allegory of spiritual union with God. In this way, he legitimizes using physical love in an allegorical fashion. Therefore, at some point, every serious believer will learn to commune with God in an intensely intimate love relationship. This is where everyone in the Church is heading, as evidenced by the bridal theme in the book of Revelation. As Ezekiel saw in his vision of water flowing from the Temple, the river of God really is too deep to ford. We just have to get to the point where we are willing to allow God to hold us by the hand and take us out over our heads; for it is in the deep waters where we become immersed in the beauty of who He is.

An explanation of how to pray this book is needed because the symbolism is difficult to interpret. The book is, of course, interactive, meaning that it contains antiphonal conversations and scenes between the Lover and the beloved (and their friends). Therefore, when praying the Song of Songs, one must first of all put oneself in a posture not only to speak to God but also to receive from Him. Much of this book is God speaking His love over us, so we must be able to see and hear in the Spirit the face and voice of the Lover. It is essential to believe the words of love that God says about us, or they will not profit us because they are not received with faith (see Heb. 4:2). For some, this will be the first hurdle to cross in praying the Song of Songs.

How should a person start to pray the Song of Songs? It is good to begin by speaking the words of the Song out loud. These words will expand one's prayer vocabulary to include words of intimacy, not just theology. They give language to the feelings of the heart through imagery and symbolism and will lead the intercessor to visualize the Lover, Christ, because they are so descriptive. Mental images of the face of Christ are encouraged so that there is actual interaction with the Person depicted in the text. The words connote an image that helps convey a thought.

In the Song of Songs, the depiction of erotic love is meant to bring us to the understanding of the progression of the spiritual life unto union. The Lover is Christ, the Bridegroom, and the Beloved is the Church (generally), or the person praying (specifically). The word picture begins to carry us into His presence and adds meaning to the otherwise abstract or theological texts of Scripture. God is, after all, love. Then, as we pray through His attributes, symbolically described in the language of love, we will see His face in different ways, as the Spirit reveals them in our hearts and minds.

What follows is a possible portrayal of how one might enter into the Song of Songs in prayer. We have chosen verse 1 of chapter 4 in the *New King James Version* to give a brief example of the imagery of the book. Start with the understanding that you are the beloved and you are listening with your heart to the words of your Lover. You listen while He speaks directly to you: "Behold, you *are* fair, my love! Behold, you *are* fair!" (emphasis added). Since you have learned the love language, you immediately know that the Father and the Son are telling you that you are cleansed, loved and accepted; that you are His bride and chosen one; that you are special to Him. Then, as you continue to verbalize what the Lover is saying about you, your Bridegroom (Lover) and you dialogue using a secret love language. He then says, "You have dove's eyes [eyes that are devoted and focused on Him] behind your veil [your heart/thoughts preserved only for your Lover]. Your hair [the symbol of your glory] is like a flock of goats, going down from Mount Gilead [symbol of beauty]".

You continue to listen as He goes on to say:

Your teeth [your smile and presence] are perfect [purified]. Your lips and mouth are lovely, beautiful and beckoning [your love and words spring from the abundance of your heart]. Your temples behind your veil [the thoughts and secret desires that you think for the Lord] are sweet like a piece of pomegranate. You have ravished my heart [I am captured with love for you] with one *look* of your eyes [simply because you have sought Me and loved Me. I am crazy about you!] (see Song of Songs 4:2-3,9, *NKJV*).

After hearing how the Lover feels about you, you begin to respond, telling Him how much you love Him. In time, a single phrase from this special love language, either from Him to you or from you to Him, will be enough to take you to a place of close communion.

Included below are some more examples of possible allegorical interpretations, so that you may have a greater understanding of the symbolism of the text.

Behold, you *are* fair [cleansed, purified, lovely, accepted], *my love* [My bride, My chosen, My elect]! Behold, you *are* fair! You *have* dove's eyes [devoted eyes, a heart focused on Me] behind your veil [modesty, you have been preserved for Me . . . your Lover]. Your hair [glory, inheritance] *is* like a flock of goats [picture of her beauty], going down from Mount Gilead [rich pastures, strong, powerful] (Song of Songs 4:1, *NKJV*, emphasis added).

Your teeth [smile, presence] *are* like a flock of shorn *sheep* which have come up from the washing [perfect, purified], every one of which bears twins, and none is barren among them [perfection, productive] (Song of Songs 4:2, *NKJV*, emphasis added).

Your lips [love, kisses] *are* like a strand of scarlet, and your mouth is lovely [beautiful, alluring, beckoning]. Your temples behind your veil [thoughts, secret desires] *are* like a piece of pomegranate [sweet, precious] (Song of Songs 4:3, *NKJV*, emphasis added).

You have ravished [captured, taken, possessed] my heart, my sister, *my* spouse [My intimate lover, now My family]; you have ravished my heart with one *look* [seeking] of your eyes [seeking Me], with one link of your necklace (Song of Songs 4:9, *NKJV*, emphasis added).

How fair [good, holy, accepted] is your love, my sister, *my* spouse! How much better than wine is your love [He enjoys her love even more than the pleasures and highs of the world, and she enjoys Him], and the scent of your perfumes [incense, prayers] than all spices! (Song of Songs 4:10, *NKJV*, emphasis added).

Your lips [kisses, words, intercession], O *my* spouse, drip as the honeycomb; honey [sweetness] and milk [softness] *are* under your tongue; and the fragrance of your garments *is* like the fragrance of Lebanon [rich, powerfully wonderful] (Song of Songs 4:11, *NKJV*, emphasis added).

A garden enclosed [reserved for the jealous One, private] *is* my sister, *my* spouse [My lover, My bride, My chosen,

My called], a spring shut up [preserved for her Lover], a fountain sealed [faithful, a virgin, devoted] (Song of Songs 4:12, *NKJV*, emphasis added).

Your plants [intimate love] *are* an orchard of pomegranates [sweet, pleasure-filled] with pleasant fruits [spiritual growth] (Song of Songs 4:13, *NKJV*, emphasis added).

As you can see, when prayed as a love story, the allegory is rich and meaningful, but it takes time and study to comprehend. We recommend that you search out a few of the great saints throughout history who have brought the subtleties of this book to life. A modern-day champion of the allegorical prayer method is Mike Bickle. For over 15 years, he has collected and studied every commentary written on the subject, so as to turn the Song of Songs into prayer. For those of you who want help, a great starting place would be to get *The Fire of Love*, a devotional prayer CD prayed by Mike Bickle, which models praying the Song of Songs from a bride's perspective. Check his website, www.fotb.com, for descriptive notes on every word of this beautiful song. Learn the love language and begin.

Beginnings of Intimacy
and Revelation

Beloved
Let him kiss me with the kisses of his mouth—
for your love is more delightful than wine.
Pleasing is the fragrance of your perfumes;
your name is like perfume poured out.
No wonder the maidens love you!

Take me away with you—let's hurry!
Let the king bring me into his chambers.

Friends
We rejoice and delight in you;
we will praise your love more than wine.

Beloved
How right they are to adore you!
Dark am I, yet lovely, O daughters of Jerusalem,
dark like the tents of Kedar, like the tent curtains of Solomon.

Do not stare at me because I am dark, darkened by the sun.
My mother's sons were angry with me
and made me take care of the vineyards;
my own vineyard I have neglected.

Tell me, you whom I love, where you graze your flock . . .
Why should I be like a veiled woman
beside the flocks of your friends?

Song of Songs 1:2-7

FAINT WITH LOVE

Lover
How beautiful you are, my darling!
Oh, how beautiful! Your eyes are doves.

Beloved
How handsome you are, my lover!
Oh, how charming! And our bed is verdant.

Lover
The beams of our house are cedars; our rafters are firs.
Beloved
I am a rose of sharon, a lily of the valleys.
Lover
Like a lily among thorns is my darling among the maidens.
Beloved
Like an apple tree among the trees of the forest
is my lover among the young men.
I delight to sit in his shade, and his fruit is sweet to my taste.
He has taken me to the banquet hall,
and his banner over me is love.

Strengthen me with raisins, refresh me with apples,
for I am faint with love.
His left arm is under my head, and his right arm embraces me.
Daughters of Jerusalem, I charge you
by the gazelles and by the does of the field:
Do not arouse or awaken love until it so desires.

Song of Songs 1:15—2:7

Embracing the Lover's Coming

Beloved
Listen! My lover! Look!

Here he comes, leaping across the mountains,
bounding over the hills.

My lover is like a gazelle or a young stag.
Look! There he stands behind our wall,
gazing through the windows,
peering through the lattice.

My lover spoke and said to me,
"Arise, my darling,
my beautiful one, and come with me.

"See!
The winter is past;
the rains are over and gone.
Flowers appear on the earth;
the season of singing has come,
the cooing of doves is heard in our land.
The fig tree forms its early fruit;
the blossoming vines spread their fragrance.

"Arise, come, my darling;
my beautiful one, come with me."

Lover

My dove in the clefts of the rock,
in the hiding places on the mountainside,
show me your face,
let me hear your voice;
for your voice is sweet, and your face is lovely.

Catch for us the foxes,
the little foxes that ruin the vineyards,
our vineyards that are in bloom.

Beloved

My lover is mine and I am his;
he browses among the lilies.
Until the day breaks and the shadows flee,
turn, my lover,
and be like a gazelle or like a young stag
on the rugged hills.

Song of Songs 2:8-17

THE DARK NIGHT OF LOVE

Beloved
All night long on my bed
I looked for the one my heart loves;
I looked for him but did not find him.

I will get up now and go about the city,
through its streets and squares;
I will search for the one my heart loves.
So I looked for him but did not find him.

The watchmen found me
as they made their rounds in the city.
"Have you seen the one my heart loves?"

Scarcely had I passed them
when I found the one my heart loves.
I held him and would not let him go
till I had brought him to my mother's house,
to the room of the one who conceived me.

Daughters of Jerusalem,
I charge you
by the gazelles and by the does of the field:
Do not arouse or awaken love
until it so desires.

Song of Songs 3:1-5

THE MIGHT OF THE LOVER

Beloved
Who is this coming up from the desert
like a column of smoke,
perfumed with myrrh and incense
made from all the spices of the merchant?

Look!
It is Solomon's carriage,
escorted by sixty warriors,
the noblest of Israel,
all of them wearing the sword,
all experienced in battle,
each with his sword at his side,
prepared for the terrors of the night.

King Solomon made for himself the carriage;
he made it of wood from Lebanon.
Its posts he made of silver,
its base of gold.
Its seat was upholstered with purple,
its interior lovingly inlaid by the daughters of Jerusalem.

Come out, you daughters of Zion,
and look at King Solomon wearing the crown,
the crown with which his mother crowned him
on the day of his wedding,
the day his heart rejoiced.

Song of Songs 3:6-11

THE BEAUTY OF THE BELOVED

Lover

All beautiful you are, my darling;
there is no flaw in you.

Come with me from Lebanon, my bride, come with me . . .

Descend from the . . . summit of Hermon,
from the lions' dens and the mountain haunts of the leopards.

You have stolen my heart, my sister, my bride;
you have stolen my heart with one glance of your eyes,

with one jewel of your necklace.

How delightful is your love,
my sister, my bride!

How much more pleasing is your love than wine,
and the fragrance of your perfume than any spice!
Your lips drop sweetness as the honeycomb, my bride;
milk and honey are under your tongue.

The fragrance of your garments is like that of Lebanon.

You are a garden locked up, my sister, my bride;

you are a spring enclosed, a sealed fountain.

You are a garden fountain,

a well of flowing water streaming down from Lebanon.

Beloved

Awake, north wind, and come, south wind!
Blow on my garden, that its fragrance may spread abroad.
Let my lover come into his garden and taste its choice fruits.

Song of Songs 4:7-12,15-16

ANTICIPATION

Beloved
I slept but my heart was awake.
Listen! My lover is knocking:
"Open to me, my sister, my darling, my dove,
my flawless one.
My head is drenched with dew,
my hair with the dampness of the night."

I have taken off my robe—must I put it on again?
I have washed my feet—must I soil them again?
My lover thrust his hand through the latch-opening;
my heart began to pound for him.

I arose to open for my lover, and my hands dripped with myrrh,
my fingers with flowing myrrh, on the handles of the lock.
I opened for my lover, but my lover had left;
he was gone.

My heart sank at his departure. I looked for him
but did not find him. I called him but he did not answer.
The watchmen found me as they made their rounds in the city.
They beat me, they bruised me; they took away my cloak,
those watchmen of the walls!

O daughters of Jerusalem,
I charge you—if you find my lover, what will you tell him?
Tell him I am faint with love.

Song of Songs 5:2-8

ALTOGETHER LOVELY

Friends
How is your beloved better than others,
most beautiful of women?
How is your beloved better than others,
that you charge us so?

Beloved
My lover is radiant and ruddy,
outstanding among ten thousand.

His head is purest gold;
his hair is wavy and black as a raven.
His eyes are like doves by the water streams,
washed in milk, mounted like jewels.
His cheeks are like beds of spice yielding perfume.
His lips are like lilies dripping with myrrh.

His arms are rods of gold set with chrysolite.
His body is like polished ivory decorated with sapphires.
His legs are pillars of marble set on bases of pure gold.
His appearance is like Lebanon, choice as its cedars.
His mouth is sweetness itself;
he is altogether lovely.

This is my lover, this my friend,
O daughters of Jerusalem.

Song of Songs 5:9-16

THE RAVISHED BRIDEGROOM

Lover
You are beautiful, my darling, as Tirzah,
lovely as Jerusalem, majestic as troops with banners.
Turn your eyes from me; they overwhelm me.

Your hair is like a flock of goats descending from Gilead.
Your teeth are like a flock of sheep coming up from the washing.
Each has its twin, not one of them is alone.

Your temples behind your veil are like . . . pomegranates.
Sixty queens there may be, and eighty concubines,
and virgins beyond number;
but my dove, my perfect one, is unique,
the only daughter of her mother, the favorite of the one
who bore her.
The maidens saw her and called her blessed;
the queens and concubines praised her.

Friends
Who is this that appears like the dawn, fair as the moon,
bright as the sun, majestic as the stars in procession?
Come back, come back, O Shulammite;
come back, come back, that we may gaze on you!

Lover
Why would you gaze on the Shulammite
as on the dance of Mahanaim?

Song of Songs 6:4-10,13

THE BRIDAL SEAL OF DIVINE FIRE

Friends
Who is this coming up from the desert leaning on her lover?
Beloved
Under the apple tree I roused you;
there your mother conceived you,
there she who was in labor gave you birth.

Place me like a seal over your heart,
like a seal on your arm; for love is as strong as death,
its jealousy unyielding as the grave.
It burns like blazing fire, like a mighty flame.
Many waters cannot quench love; rivers cannot wash it away.
If one were to give all the wealth of his house for love,
it would be utterly scorned.

Beloved
But my own vineyard is mine to give;
the thousand shekels are for you, O Solomon,
and two hundred are for those who tend its fruit.
Lover
You who dwell in the gardens with friends in attendance,
let me hear your voice!

Beloved
Come away, my lover,
and be like a gazelle or like a young stag
on the spice-laden mountains.

Song of Songs 8:5-7,12-14

Song of Songs

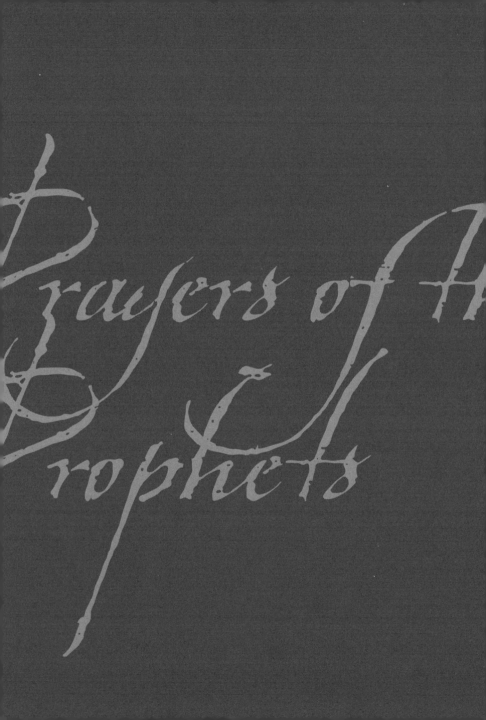

Praisers of the Prophets

PRAYERS OF THE PROPHETS

Because your sins are so many and your hostility so great, the prophet is considered a fool, the inspired man a maniac.

INTRODUCTION

Praying the prayers of the prophets opens up realms not usually touched upon in prayer. In them, more than in any other biblical text, you enter the feelings of God. It is the prophets who display, in both their lifestyles and language, the passionate emotions of the One who made us all. I have heard many people pray about knowing the heart of God. If that has ever been your desire—that you know the heart of God—then the prayers of the prophets will be your place of discovery. The prophets seem to be not only allowed but also required by God to enter into the fellowship of His sufferings (see Phil. 3:10). They are asked to feel what He feels and then to declare it to the rest of us. Think of Hosea—his whole lifestyle spoke of the suffering that a jealous God endures generation after generation—or Ezekiel, whose wife dies overnight, and Ezekiel is not even allowed to mourn as a sign to the people (see Ezek. 24:15-24). Jeremiah laments, "Oh, that my head were a spring of water and my eyes a fountain of tears!" (Jer. 9:1), so that he could weep day and night for the slain daughter of his people.

From these three biblical examples, no doubt remains in my mind that God is personal and passionate. He doesn't reside in a cranium but in the emotions and pain of everyday life. If He weren't so lovesick, our sins and idolatries would not hurt so much. But the prophets reveal that God has pain and anger, as well as pleasure and delight. God allows His servants, the prophets, to enter into His heart in a way many of us never even dream of. By praying the prayers of the prophets, we not only see the human suffering that comes from rejecting His love but also the divine suffering of He who has been, and continues to be, rejected. God's suffering is evident as He expresses, "how I have been hurt by their adulterous hearts which turned away from Me" (Ezek. 6:9, *NASB*).

The prophets section of the Bible is massive. In truth, all the biblical writers were prophets, including Moses, who wrote the Law, and David, who wrote the psalms. They saw in the Spirit; they heard the voice of God. Then, they simply announced it. Many more prayers of the prophets exist than are included here, and this brief selection only attempts to touch on the various cross-sections of life. They express the deep emotions of war, death, thankfulness, confusion, judgment and blessing. Unlike Jabez, most people are afraid to cry boldly, "Oh, that you would bless me and enlarge my territory!" (1 Chron. 4:10). In times of crisis, we often have difficulty knowing what to pray when there are real enemies, armies or terrorists. However, in prayers of the prophets, we find comfort in such times. King Jehoshaphat was able to pray with integrity, "O our God, will you not judge them? For we have no power to face this vast army that is attacking us. We do not know what to do, but our eyes are upon you" (2 Chron. 20:12). What should we do with the many imprecatory prayers of the prophets? We pray them!

Western Christianity tries to sterilize the Bible and religion. The prophets don't know anything of this. They call the proverbial spade—a spade—and they prayed that way too. The way to pray the prayers of the prophets is to see your problems and situations in light of theirs. When you are going through something, find a prayer that relates to your situation and pray it boldly. The fact that holy men have been this way before gives you confidence to speak the same words into your circumstances. For instance, if God Himself were to say to you through the greatest living prophet of your day, "You are going to die, you will not recover," you actually have biblical precedent to not accept this verdict and plead for your life (see 2 Kings 20)! Even Jesus, in the face of the most direct possible leading of God, that of His death on the cross, asked, "Father, if you are willing, take this cup from me" (Luke 22:42). Too many of us passively accept every situation (most of which are not God's will) without even asking for a different verdict.

Other than the psalms, the largest grouping of prayers that exist in the Bible are the prayers of the prophets. Once you become familiar with all the prayers that have been included here, try to find more. Inherit their promises by faith. Look for an appropriate impassioned response to every facet of life. Then branch out and pray more of the prayers of the prophets yourself.

HEAR, O ISRAEL

Hear, O Israel:
The LORD our God, the LORD is one.
[And you shall] love the LORD your God
with all your heart
and with all your soul
and with all your strength.

These commandments that I give you today
are to be upon your hearts.

Impress them on your children.
Talk about them when you sit at home
and when you walk along the road,
when you lie down and when you get up.
Tie them as symbols on your hands
and bind them on your foreheads.
Write them on the doorframes of your houses and on your gates.

When the LORD your God brings you into the land
he swore to your fathers, to Abraham, Isaac and Jacob,
to give you—a land with large, flourishing cities you did not build,
houses filled with all kinds of good things
you did not provide, wells you did not dig,
and vineyards and olive groves you did not plant—
then when you eat and are satisfied,
be careful that you do not forget the LORD,
who brought you out of Egypt, out of the land of slavery.

Deuteronomy 6:4-12

MEDITATING ON THE LAW

LORD, you have said:
"Be strong and very courageous."
So I ask for a strong and courageous heart.

Help me to be careful to obey all the law that your
servant Moses gave us;
give me the strength not to turn from it
to the right or to the left,
so that I will be successful wherever I go.

And Father, today I declare:
I will not let this *Book of the Law* depart from my mouth;
but I will meditate on it day and night.
I will pray your Law—the Bible,
out loud,
to you,
every day.
And as I pray your word,
help me to be careful to do everything written in it.
Then I will be prosperous and successful
in everything I do!

So as you have commanded me to be strong
and courageous—I pray that I will be strong!
I will not be terrified as I follow you;
I will not be discouraged as I live out my faith,
for you, O LORD, are with me wherever I go.

Joshua 1:7-9

THE PRAYER OF JABEZ—"OH, THAT YOU WOULD BLESS ME"

Now Jabez was more honorable than his brothers,

And his mother called his name Jabez,
saying, "Because I bore *him* in pain."

And Jabez called on the God of Israel saying,

"Oh, that You would bless me indeed,
and enlarge my territory,
that Your hand would be with me,
and that You would keep me from evil,
that I may not cause pain!"

So God granted him what he requested.

1 Chronicles 4:9-10, *NKJV*

FACE TO THE WALL—
"A PRAYER FOR HEALING"

In those days Hezekiah became ill and was at the point of death.
The prophet Isaiah son of Amoz went to him and said,

"This is what the LORD says:
Put your house in order, because you are going to die;
you will not recover."

Hezekiah turned his face to the wall and prayed to the LORD,
"Remember, O LORD,
how I have walked before you faithfully
and with wholehearted devotion
and have done what is good in your eyes."

And Hezekiah wept bitterly.

I said, "In the prime of my life must I go through the gates of
death and be robbed of the rest of my years?"

I said, "I will not again see the LORD,
the LORD, in the land of the living;
no longer will I look on mankind,
or be with those who now dwell in this world.

"Like a shepherd's tent my house has been pulled down
and taken from me.
Like a weaver I have rolled up my life,
and he has cut me off from the loom;
day and night you made an end of me.

"I waited patiently till dawn,
but like a lion he broke all my bones;
day and night you made an end of me.

"I cried like a swift or thrush,
I moaned like a mourning dove.
My eyes grew weak as I looked to the heavens.
I am troubled; O Lord, come to my aid!"

Before Isaiah had left the middle court,
the word of the LORD came to him:
"Go back and tell Hezekiah, the leader of my people,
'This is what the LORD, the God of your father David, says:

"'I have heard your prayer and seen your tears;
I will heal you.
On the third day from now
you will go up to the temple of the LORD.

"'I will add fifteen years to your life.
And I will deliver you and this city from the [calamity] . . . '"

[So Hezekiah praised the LORD and said:]
But what can I say?
He has spoken to me, and he himself has done this.
I will walk humbly all my years
because of this anguish of my soul.

Lord, by such things men live;
and my spirit finds life in them too.
You restored me to health and let me live.

Surely it was for my benefit that I suffered such anguish.
In your love you kept me from the pit of destruction;
you have put all my sins behind your back.

For the grave cannot praise you,
death cannot sing your praise;
those who go down to the pit cannot hope for your faithfulness.

The living, the living—they praise you, as I am doing today;
fathers tell their children about your faithfulness.

The LORD will save me,
and we will sing with stringed instruments
all the days of our lives in the temple of the LORD.

Isaiah 38:1-3,10-14; 2 Kings 20:4-6; Isaiah 38:15-20

Job's Confession

One day the angels came to present themselves before the LORD, and Satan also came with them.

The LORD said to Satan,
"Where have you come from?"
Satan answered the LORD,
"From roaming the earth and going back and forth in it."

Then the LORD said to Satan,
"Have you considered my servant Job?
There is no one on earth like him; he is blameless and upright,
a man who fears God and shuns evil."

"Does Job fear God for nothing?" Satan replied.
"Have you not put a hedge around him and his household
and everything he has? You have blessed the work of his hands,
so that his flocks and herds are spread throughout the land.
But stretch out your hand and strike everything he has,
and he will surely curse you to your face."

The LORD said to Satan,
"Very well, then, everything he has is in your hands,
but on the man himself do not lay a finger."
Then Satan went out from the presence of the LORD.

One day Job's messengers came to him and said,
your livestock has been stolen, your servants attacked,
and all your sons and daughters have been killed.

At this, Job got up and tore his robe and shaved his head.
Then he fell to the ground in worship and said:
"Naked I came from my mother's womb, and naked I will depart.
The LORD gave
and the LORD has taken away;
may the name of the LORD be praised."

And Job prayed:
I know that my Redeemer lives,
and that in the end he will stand upon the earth.
And after my skin has been destroyed,
yet in my flesh I will see God;
I myself will see him with my own eyes—I, and not another.
How my heart yearns within me!

And Job humbled himself before the LORD, and said:
"I know that you can do all things;
no plan of yours can be thwarted.
You asked,
'Who is this that obscures my counsel without knowledge?'
Surely I spoke of things I did not understand,
things too wonderful for me to know.
You said,
'Listen now, and I will speak;
I will question you, and you shall answer me.'
My ears had heard of you
but now my eyes have seen you.
Therefore I despise myself and repent in dust and ashes."

Job 1:6-21; 19:25-27; 42:2-6

Our Eyes Are on You

Some men came and told Jehoshaphat,
"A vast army is coming against you from Edom,
from the other side of the Sea.
It is already in En Gedi."

Alarmed, Jehoshaphat resolved to inquire of the LORD,
and he proclaimed a fast for all Judah.

The people of Judah came together
to seek help from the LORD;
indeed, they came from every town in Judah to seek him.

Then Jehoshaphat stood up in the assembly of Judah
and Jerusalem at the temple of the LORD
in the front of the new courtyard and said:

"O LORD, God of our fathers,
are you not the God who is in heaven?
You rule over all the kingdoms of the nations.
Power and might are in your hand,
and no one can withstand you.

"O our God,
did you not drive out the inhabitants of this land
before your people Israel
and give it forever to the descendants
of Abraham your friend?
They have lived in it
and have built in it a sanctuary for your Name, saying,

"'If calamity comes upon us,
whether the sword of judgment, or plague or famine,
we will stand in your presence
before this temple that bears your Name
and will cry out to you in our distress,
and you will hear us and save us.

"'But now here are men from [a foreign land] . . .
whose territory you would not allow Israel to invade
when they came from Egypt;
so they turned away from them and did not destroy them.

"'See how they are repaying us
by coming to drive us out of the possession
you gave us as an inheritance.

"'O our God, will you not judge them?
For we have no power to face this vast army that is attacking us.
We do not know what to do,
but our eyes are upon you.'"

Then the Spirit of the LORD came upon Jahaziel son of
Zechariah. . . .
This is what the LORD says to you:

"'Do not be afraid or discouraged because of this vast army.
For the battle is not yours, but God's.
You will not have to fight this battle.
Take up your positions;
stand firm and see the deliverance the LORD will give you.'"

2 Chronicles 20:2-12,14-15,17

THE VALLEY OF DRY BONES

The hand of the LORD was upon me,
and he brought me out by the Spirit of the LORD
and set me in the middle of a valley; it was full of bones.
He led me back and forth among them,
and I saw a great many bones on the floor of the valley,
bones that were very dry.

He asked me,
"Son of man, can these bones live?"

I said,
"O Sovereign LORD, you alone know."

Then he said to me,
"Prophesy to these bones and say to them,
'Dry bones, hear the word of the LORD!

"'This is what the Sovereign LORD says to these bones:
I will make breath enter you, and you will come to life.
I will attach tendons to you and make flesh come upon you
and cover you with skin;
I will put breath in you, and you will come to life.
Then you will know that I am the LORD.'"

So I prophesied as I was commanded.
And as I was prophesying, there was a noise, a rattling sound,
and the bones came together, bone to bone.
I looked, and tendons and flesh appeared on them
and skin covered them, but there was no breath in them.

Then he said to me,
"Prophesy to the breath;
prophesy, son of man, and say to it,

'This is what the Sovereign LORD says:
Come from the four winds, O breath,
and breathe into these slain, that they may live.'"

So I prophesied as he commanded me, and breath entered them;
they came to life and stood up on their feet—a vast army.

Then he said to me:
"Son of man, these bones are the whole house of Israel.
They say,
'Our bones are dried up and our hope is gone;
we are cut off.'

"Therefore prophesy and say to them:
'This is what the Sovereign LORD says:
O my people, I am going to open your graves
and bring you up from them;
I will bring you back to the land of Israel.
Then you, my people, will know that I am the LORD,
when I open your graves and bring you up from them.
I will put my Spirit in you and you will live,
and I will settle you in your own land.

" 'Then you will know that I the LORD have spoken,**
and I have done it, declares the LORD.'"

Ezekiel 37:1-14

INTERCESSION FOR A NATION

In the first year of Darius son of Xerxes . . .
in the first year of his reign,
I, Daniel, understood from the Scriptures,
according to the word of the LORD
given to Jeremiah the prophet,
that the desolation of Jerusalem would last seventy years.

So I turned to the Lord God
and pleaded with him in prayer and petition,
in fasting, and in sackcloth and ashes.
I prayed to the LORD my God and confessed:

"O Lord, the great and awesome God,
who keeps his covenant of love with all who love him
and obey his commands,
we have sinned and done wrong.
We have been wicked and have rebelled;
we have turned away from your commands and laws.

"We have not listened to your servants the prophets,
who spoke in your name to our kings,
our princes and our fathers,
and to all the people of the land.

"Lord, you are righteous,
but this day we are covered with shame. . . .
we are covered with shame because we have sinned against you."

"All Israel has transgressed your law and turned away,
refusing to obey you.
Therefore the curses and sworn judgments
written in the Law of Moses,
the servant of God, have been poured out on us,
because we have sinned against you.

" . . . Under the whole heaven nothing has ever been done
like what has been done to Jerusalem.
The LORD did not hesitate to bring the disaster upon us,
for the LORD our God is righteous in everything he does";
yet we have not sought the favor of the Lord our God
by turning from our sins and giving attention to your truth.

"Now, O Lord our God . . .
we have sinned, we have done wrong.
O Lord, in keeping with all your righteous acts,
turn away your anger
and your wrath from Jerusalem,
your city, your holy hill.

"Our sins and the iniquities of our fathers
have made Jerusalem and your people
an object of scorn to all those around us.

"Now, our God, hear the prayers and petitions of your servant.
For your sake, O Lord,
look with favor on your desolate sanctuary.
Give ear, O God, and hear;
open your eyes and see the desolation of the city
that bears your Name.

"We do not make requests of you because we are righteous,
but because of your great mercy.

"O Lord, listen!
O Lord, forgive!
O Lord, hear and act!
For your sake,
O my God, do not delay,
because your city
and your people bear your Name."

Daniel 9:1-8,11-12,14-19

"Thank You, God"—David's Prayer

Then King David went in and sat before the LORD,
and he said:
"Who am I, O LORD God,
and what is my family,
that you have brought me this far?

"And as if this were not enough in your sight, O God,
you have spoken about the future of the house of your servant.
You have looked on me as though
I were the most exalted of men,
O LORD God.

"What more can David say to you for honoring your servant?
For you know your servant, O LORD.
For the sake of your servant and according to your will,
you have done this great thing
and made known all these great promises.

"There is no one like you, O LORD,
and there is no God but you,
as we have heard with our own ears.

"And who is like your people Israel—
the one nation on earth
whose God went out to redeem a people for himself,
and to make a name for yourself,
and to perform great and awesome wonders
by driving out nations from before your people,
whom you redeemed from Egypt?

"You made your people Israel your very own forever,
and you, O LORD, have become their God.

"And now, LORD,
let the promise you have made
concerning your servant and his house
be established forever.

"Do as you promised,
so that it will be established
and that your name will be great forever.
Then men will say, 'The LORD Almighty,
the God over Israel, is Israel's God!'
And the house of your servant David
will be established before you.

"You, my God, have revealed to your servant
that you will build a house for him.
So your servant has found courage to pray to you.

"O LORD, you are God!
You have promised these good things to your servant.

"Now you have been pleased to bless the house of your servant,
that it may continue forever in your sight;
for you, O LORD, have blessed it,
and it will be blessed forever."

1 Chronicles 17:16-27

WHOLEHEARTED DEVOTION

David praised the LORD in the presence of the whole assembly,
saying, "Praise be to you, O LORD,
God of our father Israel, from everlasting to everlasting.

"Yours, O LORD, is the greatness and the power
and the glory and the majesty and the splendor,
for everything in heaven and earth is yours.
Yours, O LORD, is the kingdom;
you are exalted as head over all.

"Wealth and honor come from you;
you are the ruler of all things.
In your hands are strength and power
to exalt and give strength to all.

"Now, our God, we give you thanks,
and praise your glorious name.
But who am I, and who are my people,
that we should be able to give as generously as this?
Everything comes from you,
and we have given you only what comes from your hand.
We are aliens and strangers in your sight,
as were all our forefathers.
Our days on earth are like a shadow, without hope.

"O LORD our God, as for all this abundance
that we have provided for building you a temple
for your Holy Name, it comes from your hand,
and all of it belongs to you.

"I know, my God, that you test the heart
and are pleased with integrity.

"All these things have I given willingly and with honest intent.
And now I have seen with joy how willingly
your people who are here have given to you.

"O LORD, God of our fathers Abraham,
Isaac and Israel,
keep this desire in the hearts of your people forever,
and keep their hearts loyal to you.

And give my sons and daughters
the wholehearted devotion to keep your commands,
requirements and decrees
and to do everything to build the kingdom
for which I have provided."

Then David said to the whole assembly,
"Praise the LORD your God."
So they all praised the LORD,
the God of their fathers;
they bowed low and fell prostrate
before the LORD and the king.

They ate and drank with great joy
in the presence of the LORD that day.

1 Chronicles 29:10-20,22

THE AARONIC BLESSING

The LORD said to Moses,

"Tell Aaron and his sons,
'This is how you are to bless the Israelites.
Say to them:
The LORD bless you and keep you;
the LORD make his face shine upon you
and be gracious to you;
the LORD turn his face toward you
and give you peace.'

"So they will put my name on the Israelites,
and I will bless them."

Numbers 6:22-27

THE PRAYERS
OF JESUS

Heaven and earth will pass away,
but my words will never pass away.

INTRODUCTION

Every prayer of Jesus should become the prayer of every Christian. By praying the prayers of Jesus, one is engaging in the highest form of discipleship. "It is enough for the student to be like his teacher, and the servant like his master" (Matt. 10:25). Jesus not only prayed more than anyone else but His prayers also differed from all other prayers in the Bible. Although fully human, from childhood onward, He had a perfect knowledge of both the words and intent of Scripture. Thus, when in the Temple at the tender age of 12, He was able to dialogue with His teachers to such an extent that "Everyone who heard him was amazed at his understanding and his answers" (Luke 2:47). As Jesus grew, He would go to solitary places to pray (see Mark 1:35). He prayed with such intensity that it came "with loud cries and tears" (Heb. 5:7), and so earnestly that "his sweat was like drops of blood falling to the ground" (Luke 22:44). The lifestyle of prayer Jesus models for us has scarcely been touched by most Christians. But, when the prayers of Jesus are prayed back to Him, one will slowly come to realize what Jesus so obviously knew about the power of prayer. His words will lead you into His prayer experience and then into the fellowship of sonship that He Himself enjoyed with His Father.

You see, Jesus modeled a relationship with Yahweh that was radical for His day. Up to that point, no one in history had ever addressed the Lord God Almighty in the way Jesus did. Devout Jews were afraid of even using God's name, Yahweh, for fear of taking it in vain. In order to avoid this, elaborate systems were set up so Jews could refer to Yahweh without actually saying His name. Rather than pronounce the sacred name, Jews would say, "*Adonai*," which means "my Lord." As late as the medieval period, the vowels of "Adonai" were attached to the consonants *y*, *h*, *w* and *h*, resulting in the word "Jehovah." Therefore, it was quite a shock for Jesus to come from the entirely opposite end of the spectrum and address God as *Abba Pater* or Dear Daddy (see Mark 14:36). This term of endearment was nothing less than revolutionary. Even slaves could not address the head of the house as abba, because it was thought to be too personal. Normally, only infants and children used this innocent, common word for their own fathers. But never would a Jew address God in such a familiar way. So, Jesus was opening the door to an entirely new degree of intimacy when He instructed His disciples to pray, "Our Father in heaven" (Matt. 6:9). Jesus introduces us to a new relationship with God—one that resembles the intimacy and familiarity between a daddy and his child.

Jesus' prayers are also unique in that He is still praying them today. The writer to the Hebrews, encourages us by saying, "but because Jesus lives forever, he has a permanent priesthood. Therefore he is able to save completely those who come to God through him, because he always lives to intercede for them" (Heb. 7:24-25). In a very real sense, He is even praying for you right now. Jesus' prayer for Peter becomes an example of what He is praying for us now. At that time, Jesus said to Peter, "Simon,

Simon, Satan has asked [demanded for trial] to sift you [plural] as wheat. But I have prayed for you [singular], Simon, that your faith may not fail" (Luke 22:31-32). Jesus was not saying that only Peter would be tried and tested. No, He was indicating that all 12 disciples would be tried and tested and that He was praying for all 12 of them. However, He prayed for Peter in particular when He said, "I have prayed for you. . . . And when you have turned back, strengthen your brothers" (Luke 22:32). Because Jesus still lives and intercedes for us, this prayer refers to all of us who, in similar ways, are singled out for trial and testing. Who among us does not need Jesus' ongoing, continual intercession? Practically speaking, we could substitute our own names into Jesus' prayers or pray them for our own disciples. Therefore, when you pray the prayers of Jesus, you are joining with Him in His heavenly intercession. In this way, Jesus' prayers are as relevant today as when they were first prayed.

Yet there are even more ways to approach these prayers. As we begin to pray the prayers of Jesus, we start by praying the text literally, agreeing with Jesus in the historical and theological contexts of the people and things that He prayed for. When He prays for His disciples, petitioning God for this or that, you too can embrace the historical context of these prayers. Start your own prayers by simply reminding yourself of the 12 disciples who were with Him during His passionate ministry and of the Church that grew out of their testimony. When you pray the prayer of Jesus, "Glorify your Son, that your Son may glorify you" (John 17:1), you are agreeing with Jesus and continuing to pray for the manifestation of the glory of the Son. This might be a simple prayer of agreement, in which we also long for Jesus to be glorified today—that His life and passion will continue to bring glory to the Father now. In this way, we are praying today for the same things Jesus prayed for then.

At a deeper level, as the intercessor continues to pray the prayers over and over again, saying the same words that Jesus said, it becomes more apparent how Jesus thought. What was Jesus asking for? What were His concerns? By praying His words, we enter His mind and spirit—His passion. Soon His concerns become our concerns and His words our words. As this happens, we can begin to apply the same prayers to our own lives. We can also ask God to be glorified in our lives through our actions. We can ask for His will to be done in our choices. We can pray for our own families, friends and loved ones in the same way that Jesus prayed for His disciples. His concerns for His disciples were for protection and unity (see John 17:11-12), for joy in the midst of a hostile world (see John 17:13-16) and for practical holiness grown by the Word of truth (see John 17:17-19). It is a small step for any committed Christian to turn these classic texts into primary prayers for his or her own disciples. Again, we see the application of Jesus' prayers to our own personal lives.

Further, by praying the prayers of Jesus, as though they were our own prayers, we become types of Christ (anointed ones), asking these things of God for ourselves. As mentioned earlier, Jesus enjoyed a special place as the Son of God and, as such, talked to God with a boldness unknown to others. John 17 is loaded with things the average Christian would never dare utter. But as we pray the words, it slowly begins to dawn on us that, "As you [the Father] sent me [the Son] into the world, I [Jesus] have sent them [all Christians] into the world" (John 17:18). The things Jesus did we are to do because Jesus has given us the same glory that the Father gave Him (see John 17:22). Therefore, we too should glorify the Father with our lives just as Jesus did with His (see John 17:1). Since the Father granted Christ authority over all people, Jesus, by extension, is able to give His followers authority to go in His name to call others to eternal life in Christ Jesus (see Matt. 28:18). Praying Jesus' prayers imbues our spirits with the understanding that our whole lives are to be patterned after the whole of His. We also see there is work to accomplish as we move towards our own passion, when we too will be raised incorruptible with a glorious Body. The Father will glorify us when we go to be with Him (see 1 Cor. 15:40-42). Paul even prays that we would know with an intimate knowing the hope, the inheritance and the incomparably great power for us who believe. "That power is like the working of his mighty strength, which he exerted in Christ when he raised him from the dead and seated him at his right hand in the heavenly realms" (Eph. 1:19-20).

This is huge! The power that raised Jesus from the dead and brought glory to the Father is the same power that is in us now while we are alive! Praying the prayers of Jesus leads us to the place where Jesus was, the place where He intends us to go.

Eventually, in praying Jesus' prayers we find ourselves modeling our lives after His. Peter said, "To this you were called, because Christ suffered for you, leaving you an example, that you should follow in his steps" (1 Pet. 2:21). The word "example" is from the Greek compound word *hupo* which means "under," and *grammos*, meaning "writing," literally an "underwriting." The life of Jesus is the prototype, or pattern, the master copy from which we as Christians trace our lives. We are imitators of Him. And in the beginning of our Christian walk

nothing accomplishes this like substituting our names for the pronouns in Scripture, which makes praying and reciting Scripture
more personal. By filling our hearts and mouths with the very
words of Jesus, His essence forms in us. We begin to believe that we
really are Christians—"little Christ ones"—meant to live the same
supernatural, miraculous life of love that Jesus did.

Lastly, we have included "The Jesus Prayer," which grew out
of the desire to follow the biblical injunction to pray without
ceasing. It has been given different names at different times in
Church history, such as "breath prayer," "centering prayer,"
"monastic prayer" and "contemplative prayer." Although different names and nuances exist, the essence of this style of prayer
is the same. It is an extremely simple and pure form of prayer, which leads us into the presence of God. Anyone can use this
method, because it is a prayer based on experience, not intellect.
Moses once said to the Lord, "If your Presence does not go with
us, do not send us up from here" (Exod. 33:15). In one sentence,
Moses captures the longing of "The Jesus Prayer." Its desire is to
constantly remain in the felt presence of God. This lofty goal of
perpetual prayer is achieved by a very simple means. The author
of *The Cloud of Unknowing* says, "A one-syllable word such as
'God' or 'love' is best."[1] Through repeating a word or phrase over
and over again until it becomes to us as natural as breathing,
our spirits become so immersed in communion with God that
we are able to "rest in the shadow of the Almighty" (Ps. 91:1),
"abide in me . . . the vine" (John 15:4, *NKJV*) and "pray without
ceasing" (1 Thess. 5:17, *NKJV*).[2]

This method of prayer originated from the time of the
Desert Fathers and was later incorporated into the Greek
Orthodox tradition. The simple three or four phrases the Desert

Fathers chose to pray came out of a parable Jesus told in Luke 18:13. It was later changed to address the Lord Jesus, thus the title "The Jesus Prayer." The prayer is as follows: "Jesus Christ, Son of God, have mercy on me, a sinner." Nuances may change in that you may address the prayer to our Lord Jesus Christ, or you may drop the phrase "a sinner." But in the end, it is a simple phrase or thought the size of a breath, which requires focus to direct the mind in order to affect the heart and ultimately move the spirit.

An excellent illustration of this is found in *The Way of a Pilgrim*, a beautiful story of a Russian peasant seeking the answer to how to pray without ceasing. After his mentor told him to pray "The Jesus Prayer" up to 12,000 times a day, he eventually mastered it and was then swept away in God's presence. He describes his experience by saying:

> After receiving this direction, I spent the rest of the summer reciting the name of Jesus vocally and I enjoyed great peace. During my sleep I often dreamed that I was praying. And if I happened to meet people in the day they all seemed to me to be kinsmen, even though I did not know them. My thoughts had quieted down completely; I thought only of the Prayer to which my heart began to listen, and my heart produced certain warmth and gladness. . . . My solitary hut was to me like a splendid palace, and I did not know how to thank God for sending me, a great sinner, such a holy elder for a director. So now I walk and say the Jesus Prayer without ceasing, and it is more precious and sweet to me than anything else in the world. . . . I walk in a semi-conscious

state without worries, interest, and temptations. My only desire and attraction is for solitude and ceaseless recitation of the Jesus Prayer. This makes me happy. God knows what this is all about.[3]

Thus, whether we are moving toward the experience of continual communion with God by praying "The Jesus Prayer," or entering the mind of Christ through the longer, didactic prayers of Jesus, we are to follow Jesus in His prayer example. He taught us by word and deed how to pray. Therefore, every prayer of Jesus should become the prayer of every Christian.

THE LORD'S PRAYER

This, then, is how you should pray:

Our Father who is in heaven,
holy is Your name,

let Your kingdom come,
let Your will be done
on earth—as it is in heaven.

Give us today our daily bread.

Forgive us our sins,
as we forgive those who sin against us.

And lead us not into temptation,
but deliver us from the evil one.

For Yours is the kingdom
and the power
and the glory—
forever and ever.

Amen, and Amen!

Matthew 6:9-13, *NKJV*

Glorify Your Name

"Now my heart is troubled,
and what shall I say?

" 'Father, save me from this hour'?

"No, it was for this very reason
I came to this hour."

"Father, glorify your name!"

Then a voice came from heaven,
*"I have glorified it,
and will glorify it again."*

John 12:27-28

GLORIFY YOUR SON

After Jesus said this, he looked toward heaven and prayed:

"Father, the time has come.
Glorify your Son,
that your Son may glorify you.

"For you granted him authority over all people
that he might give eternal life
to all those you have given him.

"Now this is eternal life:
that they may know you,
the only true God,
and Jesus Christ,
whom you have sent.

"I have brought you glory
on earth by completing the work
you gave me to do.

"And now, Father,
glorify me in your presence
with the glory I had with you
before the world began."

John 17:1-5

A PRAYER FOR DISCIPLES

[Father,] I have revealed you to those
whom you gave me out of the world.

They were yours;
you gave them to me and they have obeyed your word.
Now they know that everything you have given me
comes from you.
For I gave them the words you gave me
and they accepted them.
They knew with certainty that I came from you,
and they believed that you sent me.

I pray for them.
I am not praying for the world,
but for those you have given me,
for they are yours.

All I have is yours,
and all you have is mine.
And glory has come to me through them.

I will remain in the world no longer,
but they are still in the world,
and I am coming to you.

Holy Father,
protect them by the power of your name—
the name you gave me—
so that they may be one as we are one.

While I was with them,
I protected them and kept them safe by that
name you gave me.
None has been lost except the one doomed to destruction
so that Scripture would be fulfilled.

I am coming to you now,
but I say these things while I am still in the world,
so that they may have the full measure of my joy
[the joy of Jesus] within them.

I have given them your word
and the world has hated them,
for they are not of the world
any more than I am of the world.

My prayer is not that you take them out of the world
but that you protect them from the evil one.
They are not of the world, even as I am not of it.

Sanctify them by the truth; your word is truth.

As you sent me into the world,
I have sent them into the world.

For them I sanctify myself,
that they too may be truly sanctified.

John 17:6-19

Unto Unity, Glory and Love

My prayer is not for them alone.
I pray also for those who will believe in me
through their message,
that all of them may be one, Father,
just as you are in me and I am in you.

May they also be in us
so that the world may believe that you have sent me.
I have given them the glory that you gave me,
that they may be one as we are one:
I in them and you in me.
May they be brought to complete unity
to let the world know that you sent me
and have loved them even as you have loved me.

Father, I want those you have given me
to be with me where I am, and to see my glory,
the glory you have given me
because you loved me before the creation of the world.

Righteous Father,
though the world does not know you, I know you,
and they know that you have sent me.
I have made you known to them,
and will continue to make you known
in order that the love you have for me may be in them
and that I myself may be in them.

John 17:20-26

WHEN YOU ARE CONVERTED

Simon, Simon,
Satan has asked to sift you as wheat.

But I have prayed for you,
Simon,
that your faith may not fail.

And when you [are converted,
and] have turned back,
strengthen your brothers.

Luke 22:31-32

YOUR WILL BE DONE

Going a little farther,
he fell with his face to the ground and prayed,

"My Father,
if it is possible,
may this cup be taken from me.
Yet not as I will,
but as you will."

Then he returned to his disciples
and found them sleeping.
"Could you men not keep watch
with me for one hour?" . . .

"Watch and pray
so that you will not fall into temptation.
The spirit is willing,
but the body is weak."

He went away a second time . . .
And being in anguish, he prayed more earnestly,
and his sweat was like drops of blood falling to the ground.

"My Father,
if it is not possible for this cup to be taken away
unless I drink it,
may your will be done."

Matthew 26:39-42; Luke 22:44; Matthew 26:42

FATHER FORGIVE THEM

When they came to the place called the Skull,
there they crucified him,
along with the criminals—
one on his right,
the other on his left.

Jesus said,
*"Father, forgive them,
for they do not know what they are doing."*

And they divided up his clothes by casting lots.

About the ninth hour Jesus cried out in a loud voice,
"Eloi, Eloi, lama sabachthani?"
—which means,
"My God, my God, why have you forsaken me?"

Jesus called out with a loud voice,
"Father, into your hands I commit my spirit."

When he had said this, he breathed his last.

Luke 23:33-34; Matthew 27:46; Luke 23:46

THE JESUS PRAYER

LORD Jesus Christ,

Son of God,

have mercy on me,

a sinner.

The Philokalia[4]

The Prophets of Lexus

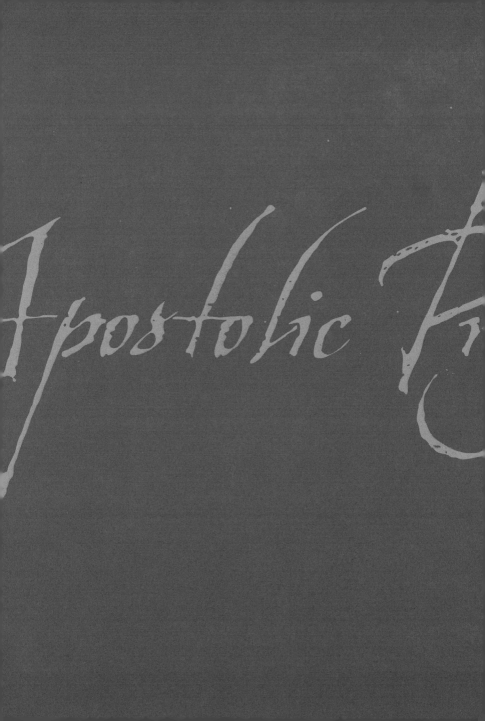

APOSTOLIC PRAYERS

I urge, then, first of all,
that requests, prayers, intercession
and thanksgiving be made for everyone.

INTRODUCTION

Have you ever listened to a father earnestly pray for his child? In the apostolic prayers, you find the apostles, the early fathers of the Church, praying for their spiritual children. Most of the apostolic prayers in the Bible were written by the apostle Paul. And Paul was, as he put it, a father: "Even though you have ten thousand guardians in Christ, you do not have many fathers, for in Christ Jesus I became your father through the gospel" (1 Cor. 4:15). Therefore, in these prayers you hear a father praying, which is a different form of prayer than is found anywhere else in the Bible.

As one of the most pharisaical Jews in history, Paul was eminently endowed with the credentials to create a new prayer genre. His life had been devoted to *meditating on the Law day and night* (see Josh. 1:8). He would have known the psalms almost by heart. He studied the Torah and the traditions so intricately that he burned with murderous zeal against those who opposed them. Then he had the cataclysmic, personal revelation of Messiah, complete with the proverbial "knocked off your horse" experience. This new revelation did not detract from his lifelong learning—it only added to it! Moreover, Paul received numerous visions and revelations directly from the Spirit of God. As a result, when Paul prays, he prays as one rooted and grounded in the historical faith of his fathers, yet with the full understanding of the Messiah, whom all of the prophets had been waiting for.

As Abraham was the father of all who believe, so Paul, Peter and John became fathers of the apostolic faith. Hence, the apostolic prayers are fatherly prayers. They express what a father wants for those he has helped birth and is raising in the Lord. They are filled with love, longing and wisdom. Sprinkled with words of affection, the tone of these prayers is often pastoral and tender. These fathers condense lessons learned from a life of following Jesus and intercede specifically for the things that they know will be the most difficult, or most necessary, for their sons and daughters in a given region. If parents today were to stop and write down their desires for their children, they would find their expressions echoed in the apostolic prayers. Only, the apostolic prayers would express these desires far better than any parent ever could, because they were originally inspired from the heart of our Father God.

The apostolic prayers are also foundational prayers. As founders of the Church, the apostles were setting things in order. They were grounding the disciples of Jesus in the essential theological basics that children of God need to know in order to grow in their spiritual life. Therefore, they include necessary truths, not flowery extras. They focus on character, the knowledge of God and the power of the Spirit-filled life. Because of this, they are easily applicable to our lives today. For example, many people pray to know God's will in their lives. They ask whether they should take this job or that job, whether they should go here or go there. Yet when one prays the apostolic prayers, the emphasis is different. In the Bible, being filled with the knowledge of God's will includes such things as "bearing fruit in every good work" (Col. 1:10). The will of God, in the biblical sense, is not so much about going to this location or that location but rather about bearing fruit *while* we are going. The emphasis on following the will of God in the apostolic prayers is whether we are actually getting to know God better. If not, then we are probably out of His will. Further, the understanding of "bearing fruit" includes good works, discipleship and character issues. Through consistent apostolic praying, we will sort out much of the chatter and misapplication of our contemporary, biblically illiterate prayers.

The apostolic prayers have several features that are worth noting. A primary consideration is that they are God focused. They are, in fact, so God focused that they virtually ignore the demonic hosts. The apostolic prayers never address Satan, either to rebuke him or bind him. When the apostles prayed, they prayed directly to the Father and asked Him to deal with any obstacles that might have been standing in the way of their prayers. They directed their appeals to the Father, in the name of the Son, for answers generated by the power of the Holy Spirit. This does not mean that we cannot follow Jesus' or Paul's examples of rebuking sin, sickness and demonic spirits. As Mike Bickle says,

> The Holy Spirit on specific occasions may lead the Church to war against a principality. I see this as a governmental function requiring unity among those in spiritual authority. Such strategic warfare is divinely orchestrated by the Holy Spirit on prophetic occasions.[1]

Yet such is not the case with the apostolic prayers; rather, their predominant pattern is to appeal to the Father to see things accomplished in the Church. Thus the way is open for the Holy Spirit to convict the world of sin, righteousness and judgment.

In addition to the God focus, apostolic prayers are positive prayers. They ask that we would be filled with good things, that we would prosper and that we would increase in the knowledge of God. Apostolic prayers are not focused on fixing what we are not but rather on fulfilling what we can be. For example, rather than telling God how bad everything is and how rotten the world is getting, these prayers ask for our joy to increase and grace to abound. Instead of preaching prayers that tell everyone else what they ought to do, apostolic prayers speak directly to God, asking Him to accomplish His desired goals. They petition Him for people to be filled with the Holy Spirit and for the Church to flourish through the manifestation of the gifts and fruits of the Spirit (i.e., the preaching of the word, prophetic revelation, signs and wonders, love, unity, etc.). Such positive prayers beget positive results.

Finally, apostolic prayers are mostly for the Church. They bring before God the concerns of the saved, whether individuals, churches or regions. Apostolic prayers are meant to be prayed with someone, or some place, specifically in mind. These are not "God bless the whole wide world" prayers! When praying these prayers for yourself, personalize them by changing the pronouns, and ask that God would do work in your own life. Then pray the exact same words over your friends and family, putting their names in the text. Do the same for your church and the other churches throughout your city or region. When you do this, you will be praying like the apostles prayed. You can even expect the same results!

Since apostolic prayers are for the Church, they're almost exclusively for the saved. This is a significant point, considering how many intercessors only want to pray for the lost and, in doing so, disregard the Church. A dangerous tendency exists for intercessors to become discouraged and angry with the Church and to begin to concentrate their prayers almost exclusively on the lost. But apostolic prayers focus on the Church, to the end that Christians become filled with the power and gifts of God so that they—as empowered ones—will reach the lost. This is how Jesus Himself taught us to pray. He said, "The harvest is plentiful but the workers are few. Ask the Lord of the harvest, therefore, to send out workers into his harvest field" (Matt. 9:37-38). While we are called to love our neighbor, apostolic prayers ensure that we don't neglect our spiritual family.

All that remains, then, is to pray the apostolic prayers. Although this sounds easy enough, you will not be long into praying before you discover that every word is packed with meaning. We suggest that you pray them slowly, phrase by phrase, or even word by word, until you know the exact meaning and intent of each word. Stop and ruminate on the depth of what is being asked for, and keep a commentary handy for those easily misunderstood theological concepts. As Peter said, "[Paul's] letters contain some things that are hard to understand" (2 Pet. 3:16). As with all prayer, you cannot pray well when you don't know what you are asking for. So take your time. Pray slowly. Look up words and concepts you don't understand. And, above all else, ask the Father to give you, through these prayers, a revelation of His heart.

Revival Power

When they heard this,
they raised their voices together in prayer to God.
"Sovereign Lord," they said,
"you made the heaven and the earth and the sea,
and everything in them.
You spoke by the Holy Spirit
through the mouth of your servant, our father David:

" 'Why do the nations rage and the peoples plot in vain?
The kings of the earth take their stand
and the rulers gather together
against the Lord and against his Anointed One.'

"Indeed they have conspired against your holy servant Jesus,
whom you anointed.
They did what your power and will
had decided beforehand should happen.

"Now, Lord, consider their threats
and enable your servants to speak your word with great boldness.
Stretch out your hand to heal
and perform miraculous signs and wonders
through the name of your holy servant Jesus."

After they prayed, the place where they were meeting was shaken.
And they were all filled with the Holy Spirit
and spoke the word of God boldly.

Acts 4:24-31

Revival of Divine Revelation

For this reason,
ever since I heard about your faith
in the Lord Jesus
and your love for all the saints,

I have not stopped giving thanks for you,
remembering you in my prayers.

I keep asking that the God of our Lord Jesus Christ,
the glorious Father,
may give you the Spirit of wisdom and revelation,
so that you may know him better.

I pray also
that the eyes of your heart may be enlightened
in order that
you may know the hope to which he has called you,
the riches of his glorious inheritance in the saints,
and his incomparably great power for us who believe.

That power is like the working of his mighty strength,
which he exerted in Christ
when he raised him from the dead
and seated him at his right hand
in the heavenly realms.

Ephesians 1:15-20

THE OUTPOURING OF DIVINE LOVE

For this reason I kneel before the Father,
from whom his whole family in heaven
and on earth derives its name.

I pray that out of his glorious riches
he may strengthen you with power
through his Spirit in your inner being,
so that Christ may dwell in your hearts through faith.
And I pray that you,
being rooted and established in love,
may have power, together with all the saints,
to grasp how wide
and long
and high
and deep
is the love of Christ,
and to know this love that surpasses knowledge—
that you may be filled to the measure
of all the fullness of God.

Now to him who is able to do immeasurably more
than all we ask or imagine,
according to his power that is at work within us,
to him be glory in the church and in Christ Jesus
throughout all generations,
for ever and ever!
Amen.

Ephesians 3:14-21

THE RELEASE OF PROPHETIC BOLDNESS

And pray in the Spirit . . .
with all kinds of prayers
and requests.

With this in mind,
be alert and always keep on praying
for all the saints.

Pray also for me,
that whenever I open my mouth,
words may be given me
so that I will fearlessly
make known the mystery of the gospel,
for which I am an ambassador in chains.

Pray that I may declare it fearlessly,
as I should.

Ephesians 6:18-20

OVERFLOWING HOLY LOVE

I thank my God every time I remember you.

In all my prayers for all of you,
I always pray with joy.

And this is my prayer:
that your love may abound
more and more
in knowledge and depth of insight,
so that
you may be able to discern
what is best
and may be pure
and blameless
until the day of Christ,

filled with the fruit of righteousness
that comes through Jesus Christ—
to the glory and praise of God.

Philippians 1:3-4,9-11

FILLED WITH A KNOWLEDGE OF HIS WILL

To the holy and faithful brothers in Christ at Colosse:
Grace and peace to you from God our Father.
We always thank God, the Father of our Lord Jesus Christ,
when we pray for you,
because we have heard of your faith in Christ Jesus
and of the love you have for all the saints—

For this reason, since the day we heard about you,
we have not stopped praying for you and
asking God to fill you with the knowledge of his will
through all spiritual wisdom and understanding.

And we pray this in order that
you may live a life worthy of the Lord
and may please him in every way:
bearing fruit in every good work,
growing in the knowledge of God,

being strengthened with all power
according to his glorious might
so that you may have great endurance
and patience,
and joyfully giving thanks to the Father,

who has qualified you to share in the
inheritance of the saints in the kingdom of light.

Colossians 1:2-4,9-12

THE DOOR OF GOD

Devote yourselves to prayer,
being watchful and thankful.

And pray for us, too,
that
God may open a door
for our message,
so that we may proclaim
the mystery of Christ,
for which I am in chains.

Pray that I may proclaim it clearly,
as I should.

Also, I,
who am one of you and a servant of Christ Jesus,
send you greetings.

I am always wrestling in prayer for you,
that you may stand firm in all the will of God,
mature and fully assured.

Colossians 4:2-4,12

THE ESTABLISHED HEART

How can we thank God enough for you
in return for all the joy we have
in the presence of our God because of you?
Night and day we pray most earnestly
that we may see you again
and supply what is lacking in your faith.

*Now may our God and Father himself
and our Lord Jesus clear the way for us to come to you.*

*May the Lord
make your love increase and overflow for each other
and for everyone else, just as ours does for you.*

*May he strengthen [and establish] your hearts
so that you will be blameless and holy
in the presence of our God and Father
when our Lord Jesus comes with all his holy ones.*

*May God himself, the God of peace,
sanctify you through and through.
May your whole spirit, soul and body
be kept blameless at the coming of our Lord Jesus Christ.*

The one who calls you is faithful
and he will do it.
Brothers, pray for us.

1 Thessalonians 3:9-13; 5:23-25

FULFILL YOUR CALL

We ought always to thank God for you, brothers, and rightly so,

because your faith is growing more and more,
and the love every one of you has for each
other is increasing.

With this in mind,
we constantly pray for you,

that our God may count you worthy of his calling,
and that by his power
he may fulfill every good purpose of yours
and every act prompted by your faith.

We pray this so that the name of our Lord Jesus
may be glorified in you,
and you in him,
according to the grace of our God
and the Lord Jesus Christ.

2 Thessalonians 1:3,11-12

INCREASE YOUR WORD

Finally, brothers,
pray for us that the message of the Lord
may spread rapidly
and be honored,
just as it was with you.

And pray that we may be delivered
from wicked and evil men,
for not everyone has faith.

But the Lord is faithful,
and he will strengthen
and protect you from the evil one.

May the Lord direct your hearts into God's love
and Christ's perseverance.

Now may the Lord of peace himself give you peace
at all times and in every way.

The Lord be with all of you.

2 Thessalonians 3:1-3,5,16

Just Say No!

For the grace of God that brings salvation
has appeared to all men.

It teaches us to say
"No"
to ungodliness
and worldly passions,

and to live self-controlled,
upright
and godly lives
in this present age,

while we wait for the blessed hope—
the glorious appearing
of our great God
and Savior, Jesus Christ.

Titus 2:11-13

A Prayer of Prosperity

Dear friend,
I pray that you may enjoy good health

and that in all respects,
everything may go well with you,
even as your soul is getting along well.

That you may prosper in all things,
just as your soul prospers.

3 John 1:2

Jude's Doxology

To him
who is able to keep you from falling
and to present you [standing]
before his glorious presence
without fault and with great joy—

to the only God our Savior
be glory,
majesty,
power
and authority,

through Jesus Christ our Lord,
before all ages,
now and forevermore!

Amen.

Jude 1:24-25

THE APOSTOLIC BENEDICTION

Finally, brothers,
good-by.

Aim for perfection,
listen to my appeal,
be of one mind,
live in peace.

And the God of love and peace
will be with you.

Greet one another with a holy kiss.

All the saints send their greetings.

May the grace of the Lord Jesus Christ,
and the love of God,
and the fellowship of the Holy Spirit
be with you all.

2 Corinthians 13:11-14

HYMNS OF THE REVELATION

Blessed is the one who reads the word of this prophecy, and blessed are those who hear it and take to heart what is written in it, because the time is near.

INTRODUCTION

In life, when you don't know the outcome of a given trial, you may be tempted to quit in the middle. That is why the book of the Revelation of Jesus Christ—in which Jesus is revealed as the totally triumphant, conquering King of kings—must become an integral part of every believer's prayer life. John begins the book saying that the one who reads and hears the words of this prophecy is blessed (see Rev. 1:3). Having had a series of visions of what lay ahead for the Church, John knew what was coming. He knew the future would not be easy, but he also knew the final outcome. He echoes the last sentiments of Jesus to the apostles: "In this world you will have trouble. But take heart! I have overcome the world" (John 16:33).

Praying the hymns of the Revelation will give faith to every suffering Christian, perspective to every unjust situation and hope to everyone who feels like giving up. Weak people will overcome difficult situations, because praying the hymns reveals to us what is going on in the eternal world while we live life in the temporal one. In the book of Revelation, we have gone back to the future; thus, our vantage point on the present is different. Regardless of one's theological interpretation of the book, all things ultimately conclude with the bodily return of Jesus

Christ and the coming of a new heaven and new Earth (see Rev. 19–22). To that end, we pray these prayers with a coming of, forward-looking emphasis. No matter what your state on Earth now, things are going to get better. We have a real future and a real hope.

A distinct feature of the hymns of the Revelation is that they reveal the attitude of heaven toward the judgments of God on Earth. Heaven is not neutral to these judgments. In fact, there is vigorous agreement with all created order that justice has come at last. The martyrs cry out, "How long, Sovereign Lord, holy and true, until you . . . avenge our blood?" (Rev. 6:10). The angel with the bowl of wrath says, "they poured out the blood of saints and prophets, and Thou hast given them blood to drink. They deserve it" (Rev. 16:6, *NASB*). To which the altar responds, "true and righteous are Thy judgments" (Rev. 16:7, *NASB*). The elders declare, "The time has come for judging the dead . . . and for destroying those who destroy the earth" (Rev. 11:18). Most of us would normally not say these types of prayers. But heaven says them; therefore, we must say them too. Regularly praying heaven's prayers aligns us with heaven's perspective—a perspective that shows us that God is making all wrongs right. Finally, He is bringing an end to sin and sorrow. Finally, He wins the war. In the word of the living creatures, "Amen!"

Therefore, heaven is not characterized as sad. Heaven is jubilant, victorious and exultant, which is why the hymns must be prayed "out loud and loud." Repeatedly throughout Revelation, John shows us that heavenly worship is not only out loud, it is also loud! Over 22 times, John notes that the praise, prayers and declarations of the angels in heaven are loud. In heaven, speech is described as being like the roar of a lion, the crash of an ocean or a bang like thunder. The seven thunders of judgment are said to have spoken (see Rev. 10:3-4). Why is everything loud? What is the reason for the volume? Why do people and angels and living creatures sing, shout, praise and declare so loudly?

Simply stated, the reason is passion! Passion is at the root of praying "out loud and loud." Because of fear, a timid mother cries out. Anger makes a parent loud. Excitement causes a crowd to roar. Victory enables an army to shout. Affirmation makes a fan cheer. Joy entices a group to yell. Behind each of these emotions is passion, and passion incites loudness. Conversely, if someone is bored, depressed or passionless, he or she is usually quiet. But it takes focus and energy to have volume in your voice. It's hard to be loud if you are not into it, because loudness takes effort. What do those in heaven see that gives them so much inspiration? Obviously, something about the unobstructed, face-to-face encounter with God blows away any bored, lackadaisical attitudes. Does it say something about our feelings toward God when we will not lift up our voice on Earth? Simply put, our own inability to pray "out loud and loud" exposes a deficiency of passion, because loudness is part of loving God with all our soul and strength.

Many people, particularly in the Western world, have a distinct aversion to praying "out loud and loud." Why? Because they most likely do not know what to say, and they are not really into it. Thus, silent prayers come to mind by default. Even if people do have the words—in the form of a psalm, hymn or prayer—their prayers often feel flat and lifeless. However, just praying the Bible, and doing it *loudly*, can affect your passion and vice versa. Even when you may not feel into it, as you discipline your soul to "stand up and praise the LORD" (Neh. 9:5), zeal and encouragement will invariably take over.

This principle is also true in our daily lives. Usually when people talk about certain subjects, passionate feelings are evoked. So when it comes to the issue of prayer, the questions should be asked: Do you pray out loud to God because you are into it? Or do you pray out loud by faith, feeling nothing, and trust that God is hearing and will answer? Of course, the answer is both. We come to God by faith, and the practical bonus of praying "out loud and loud" is that we are eventually impacted by what we say. Our emotions will be affected if we discipline our wills to give a sacrifice of praise. All too often we are led by the impulses of the moment. If we don't feel excited, passionate or zealous in spirit at that moment, we tend not to stir ourselves to actually give the sacrifice of praise. However, when it comes to prayer, we do not have to passively wait for the waters to be stirred. We can stir them ourselves just by praying "out loud and loud!"

This is especially true when praying the hymns of the Revelation, because the words of these hymns are packed with emotion. As you pray them, you will discover at least 10 worship words. The worship words are short, strong words such as "power," "wealth," "wisdom," "strength," "honor," "glory," "praise," "blessing," "might" and "dominion" (see Rev. 1:6; 5:12; 7:12). There are also five victory chants: "Holy, Holy, Holy" (Rev. 4:8); "Worthy is the Lamb" (Rev. 5:12); "Salvation belongs to our God" (Rev. 7:10); "Great and marvelous" and "Just and true" (Rev. 15:3). In addition to these, numerous other titles and banners praise and exalt God and the Lamb.

The inspiration of these words will lead you right into God's presence. One way to pray these hymns is to imagine that your voice is your instrument and that these words are your notes. Imagine that each of the worship words or victory chants creates a different note in heaven, even when it is shouted and not sung. For example, the word "power" would sound different from "wealth." "Wisdom" would make a different sound from that of "strength." And "honor," "glory" and "praise" are different from "blessing," "thanks" and "dominion." With this in mind, then, lift up your "voice like a trumpet" (Isa. 58:1; Rev. 1:10), and send your own worship to the courts of heaven. In this way, as we shout the words to Him, it is as though we are playing a worship song, spiritually speaking. And, every time we do it, each word sounds beautiful in His ears. This is what the angels do. These words are heaven's response to the raw revelation of God.

So, as we worship in this way, these staccato-like shouts will also encourage those in the gathering with us to shout exultant praise to God. Our worship will invite others to join us, as we ourselves join with the hosts of heaven. Think of it—the angels, the martyrs, the end-time harvest, the 144,000, the great multitude in heaven, the 24 elders, the living creatures and the entire heavenly host—all worshiping God together with us! Remember, no one in heaven is quiet. So when you pray the hymns of the revelation "out loud and loud," you will be praying on Earth just as they do in heaven! It's the next best thing to being there.

LOOK . . . HE IS COMING!

John, To the seven churches in the province of Asia:
Grace and peace to you
from him who is,
and who was,
and who is to come,
and from the seven spirits before his throne,
and from Jesus Christ,
who is the faithful witness,
the firstborn from the dead,
and the ruler of the kings of the earth.

To him who loves us and has freed us
from our sins by his blood,
and has made us to be a kingdom and priests
to serve his God and Father—
to him be glory
and power
for ever and ever!
Amen.

Look, he is coming with the clouds,
and every eye will see him,
even those who pierced him;
and all the peoples of the earth will mourn
because of him.
So shall it be!
Amen.

Revelation 1:4-7

THE OVERCOMER'S PRAYER

. . . These are the words of him
who holds the seven stars in his right hand
and walks among the seven golden lampstands:

He who has an ear,
let him hear what the Spirit says to the churches.

To him who overcomes, I will give the right
to eat from the tree of life, which is in the paradise of God.

. . . These are the words of him who is the
First and the Last, who died and came to life again.

He who has an ear,
let him hear what the Spirit says to the churches.

He who overcomes
will not be hurt at all by the second death.

. . . These are the words of him
who has the sharp, double-edged sword.

He who has an ear,
let him hear what the Spirit says to the churches.

To him who overcomes,
I will give some of the hidden manna.
I will also give him a white stone with a new name written on
it, known only to him who receives it.

. . . These are the words of the Son of God,
whose eyes are like blazing fire
and whose feet are like burnished bronze.

He who has an ear,
let him hear what the Spirit says to the churches.

To him who overcomes
and does my will to the end,
I will give authority over the nations—
He will rule them with an iron scepter;
he will dash them to pieces like pottery—
just as I have received authority from my Father.
I will also give him the morning star.

. . . These are the words of him
who holds the seven spirits of God
and the seven stars.

He who has an ear,
let him hear what the Spirit says to the churches.

He who overcomes will, like them,
be dressed in white.
I will never blot out his name from the book of life,
but will acknowledge his name before my Father
and his angels.

He who has an ear,
let him hear what the Spirit says to the churches.

. . . These are the words of him who is holy and true,
who holds the key of David.
What he opens no one can shut,
and what he shuts no one can open.

Him who overcomes
I will make a pillar in the temple of my God.
Never again will he leave it.
I will write on him the name of my God
and the name of the city of my God,
the new Jerusalem,
which is coming down out of heaven from my God;
and I will also write on him my new name.

. . . These are the words of the Amen,
the faithful and true witness, the ruler of God's creation.

To him who overcomes,
I will give the right to sit with me on my throne,
just as I overcame
and sat down with my Father on his throne.

He who has an ear,
let him hear what the Spirit says to the churches.

Revelation 2:1,7-8,11-12,17-18,26-29; 3:1,5-7,12,14,21-22

Holy, Holy, Holy!

Each of the four living creatures had six wings
and was covered with eyes all around,
even under his wings.
Day and night they never stop saying:
"Holy, holy, holy is the Lord God Almighty,
who was,
and is,
and is to come."

Whenever the living creatures
give glory, honor and thanks
to him who sits on the throne
and who lives
for ever and ever,
the twenty-four elders fall down
before him who sits on the throne,
and worship him who lives for ever and ever.

They **lay their crowns before the throne and say:**
"You are worthy, our Lord and God,
to receive glory
and honor
and power,
for you created all things,
and by your will
they were created
and have their being."

Revelation 4:8-11

WORTHY IS THE LAMB

And when he [the Lion of the tribe of Judah]
had taken it [the scroll
from the right hand of him who sat on the throne],
the four living creatures and the twenty-four elders
fell down before the Lamb.

Each one had a harp
and they were holding golden bowls full of incense,
which are the prayers of the saints.

And they sang a new song:
"You are worthy to take the scroll and to open its seals,
because you were slain,
and with your blood you purchased men for God
from every tribe and language and people and nation.

"You have made them
to be a kingdom and priests
to serve our God,
and they will reign on the earth."

Then I looked
and heard the voice of many angels,
numbering thousands upon thousands,
and ten thousand times ten thousand.

They encircled the throne and the living creatures and the elders.

In a loud voice they sang:
"Worthy is the Lamb, who was slain,
to receive power
and wealth
and wisdom
and strength
and honor
and glory
and praise!"

Then I heard every creature in heaven
and on earth
and under the earth
and on the sea,
and all that is in them,
singing:
"To him who sits on the throne and to the Lamb
be praise
and honor
and glory
and power,
for ever and ever!"

The four living creatures said,
"Amen,"
and the elders fell down and worshiped.

Revelation 5:8-14

THE MARTYR'S CRY

When he opened the fifth seal,
I saw under the altar the souls
of those who had been slain
because of the word of God
and the testimony they had maintained.

They called out in a loud voice,
"How long,
Sovereign Lord, holy and true,
until you judge the inhabitants of the earth
and avenge our blood?"
[How long?]

Then each of them was given a white robe,
and they were told to wait a little longer,
until the number of their fellow servants and brothers
who were to be killed
as they had been killed was completed.

Revelation 6:9-11

PRAISE OF THE END-TIME HARVEST

After this I looked
and there before me was a great multitude
that no one could count,
from every nation, tribe, people and language,
standing before the throne
and in front of the Lamb.

They were wearing white robes
and were holding palm branches in their hands.

And they cried out in a loud voice:
"Salvation belongs to our God,
who sits on the throne,
and to the Lamb."

All the angels were standing around the throne
and around the elders and the four living creatures.
They fell down on their faces before the throne
and worshiped God, saying:
"Amen!
Praise
and glory
and wisdom
and thanks
and honor
and power
and strength
be to our God for ever and ever.
Amen!"

Then one of the elders asked me,
"These in white robes—
who are they,
and where did they come from?"

I answered,
"Sir, you know."

And he said,
"These are they
who have come out of the great tribulation;
they have washed their robes
and made them white in the blood of the Lamb."

Therefore,
"they are before the throne of God
and serve him day and night in his temple;
and he who sits on the throne will spread his tent over them.

"Never again will they hunger;
never again will they thirst.
The sun will not beat upon them,
nor any scorching heat.

"For the Lamb at the center of the throne
will be their shepherd;
he will lead them to springs of living water.
And God will wipe away every tear from their eyes."

Revelation 7:9-17

TIME TO REIGN

The seventh angel sounded his trumpet,
and there were loud voices in heaven,
which said:
"The kingdom of the world
has become the kingdom
of our Lord and of his Christ,
and he will reign for ever and ever."

And the twenty-four elders,
who were seated on their thrones before God,
fell on their faces and worshiped God, saying:

"We give thanks to you,
Lord God Almighty,
the One who is and who was,
because you have taken your great power
and have begun to reign.

"The nations were angry;
and your wrath has come.

"The time has come for judging the dead,
and for rewarding your servants the prophets
and your saints and those who reverence your name,
both small and great—
and for destroying those who destroy the earth."

Revelation 11:15-18

OVERCOMING THE DRAGON

Then I heard a loud voice in heaven say:
"Now have come
the salvation
and the power
and the kingdom of our God,
and the authority of his Christ.

"For the accuser of our brothers,
who accuses them before our God day and night,
has been hurled down.

"They overcame him
by the blood of the Lamb
and by the word of their testimony;
they did not love their lives so much
as to shrink from death.

"Therefore rejoice, you heavens
and you who dwell in them!
But woe to the earth and the sea,
because the devil has gone down to you!
He is filled with fury,
because he knows that his time is short."

Revelation 12:10-12

THE SONG OF MOSES

And I saw what looked like a sea of glass
mixed with fire
and, standing beside the sea,
those who had been victorious
over the beast and his image
and over the number of his name.

They held harps given them by God
and sang the song of Moses the servant of God
and the song of the Lamb:

"Great and marvelous are your deeds,
Lord God Almighty.
Just and true are your ways,
King of the ages.

"Who will not fear you, O Lord,
and bring glory to your name?
For you alone are holy.
All nations will come and worship before you,
for your righteous acts have been revealed."

Revelation 15:2-4

JUST AND TRUE

Then I heard a loud voice from the temple
saying to the seven angels,
"Go, pour out the seven bowls of God's wrath on the earth."

Then I heard the angel in charge of the waters say:

"You are just in these judgments,
you who are and who were,
the Holy One,
because you have so judged;

"for they have shed the blood
of your saints and prophets, and
you have given them blood to drink
as they deserve."

And I heard the altar respond:
"Yes, Lord God Almighty,
true and just are your judgments."

Revelation 16:1,5-7

THE WEDDING SONG

After this I heard what sounded like the roar
of a great multitude in heaven shouting:
"Hallelujah!
Salvation and glory and power belong to our God,
for true and just are his judgments.
He has condemned the great prostitute
who corrupted the earth by her adulteries.
He has avenged on her the blood of his servants."

And again they shouted:
"Hallelujah! The smoke from her goes up for ever and ever."

The twenty-four elders and the four living creatures
fell down and worshiped God, who was seated on the throne.
And they cried:
"Amen, Hallelujah!"
Then a voice came from the throne, saying:
"Praise our God, all you his servants,
you who fear him, both small and great!"

Then I heard what sounded like a great multitude—
like the roar of rushing waters and like loud peals
of thunder, shouting:
"Hallelujah! For our Lord God Almighty reigns.
Let us rejoice and be glad and give him glory!
For the wedding of the Lamb has come,
and his bride has made herself ready.
Fine linen, bright and clean, was given her to wear."

Revelation 19:1-8

COME, LORD JESUS!

"Behold, I am coming soon!
My reward is with me,
and I will give to everyone according to what he has done.
I am the Alpha and the Omega, the First and the Last,
the Beginning and the End.
Blessed are those who wash their robes,
that they may have the right to the tree of life
and may go through the gates into the city.
Outside are the dogs, those who practice magic arts,
the sexually immoral, the murderers, the idolaters
and everyone who loves and practices falsehood.

"I, Jesus, have sent my angel
to give you this testimony for the churches.
I am the Root and the Offspring of David,
and the bright Morning Star."
The Spirit and the bride say,
"Come!"
And let him who hears say,
"Come!"
Whoever is thirsty,
let him come;
and whoever wishes,
let him take the free gift of the water of life.
He who testifies to these things says,
"Yes, I am coming soon."
Amen. Come, Lord Jesus.

Revelation 22:12-17,20

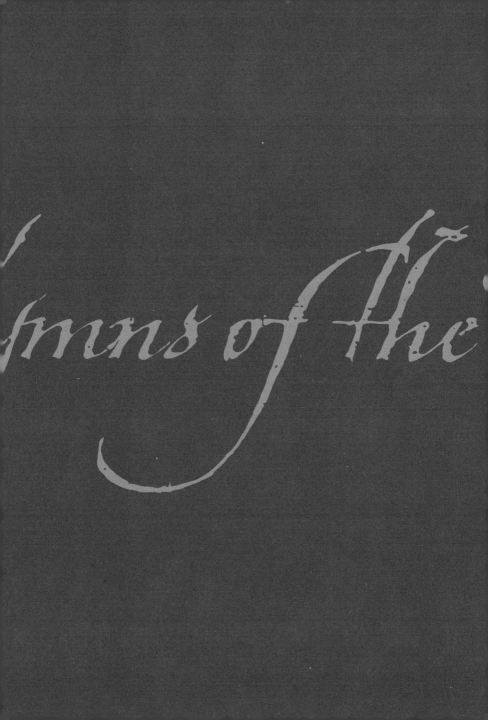

ORGANIZATIONAL "PRAYING THE BIBLE" PRAYER CHART

EXPLANATION

We have included this chart to help you get in the habit of praying the Bible. There is an important philosophy behind it. We have found that everybody needs structure and that good habits are formed through repetition and consistency. For centuries, the people of God engaged in the regular routine of praying the Bible. When you form the habit, the habit forms you.

Children, in particular, need to be taught to pray. In working with our own children for over three years, we have discovered that unless something is in place children can easily follow, the practice dissipates. A daily chart, which they can fill out and bring to you, will not only help them form a habit, it will also put the onus on them to get it done. While it makes the prayer time fun, it also forms a good habit. Younger children will benefit greatly by getting it signed by a parent every day.

We also want to underscore the idea of privilege versus punishment. The intention is not to punish children for not saying their prayers. Yet it is very biblical to withhold privileges. In our household, the way we have worked it is summed up like this: "Pray today, play tomorrow. No pray? No play!" If they forget to pray, they lose a privilege; however, when they have filled out a chart, we reward them. Children like to be rewarded for their efforts.

The chart is fairly self-explanatory. All you need to do is photocopy it, insert the dates, check off which section of prayers has been prayed and write down the specific verses of text. Adults and children alike can use the chart to regain the lost art of daily prayers.

Organizational "Praying the Bible" Prayer Chart

Name: _____

Week of: _____

WEEKDAYS			
Prayer Categories	MONDAY Today I prayed... ☑ Text	TUESDAY Today I prayed... ☑ Text	WEDNESDAY Today I prayed... ☑ Text
Theophanies	❑	❑	❑
Psalms	❑	❑	❑
Wisdom	❑	❑	❑
Songs	❑	❑	❑
Prophets	❑	❑	❑
Jesus	❑	❑	❑
Apostolic	❑	❑	❑
Hymns	❑	❑	❑
Extra Prayers	❑	❑	❑
Prayed # Min.	min.	min.	min.
Today I felt...			

W E E K	D A Y S		
THURSDAY	FRIDAY	SATURDAY	SUNDAY
Today I prayed...	*Today I prayed...*	*Today I prayed...*	*Today I prayed...*
☑ Text	☑ Text	☑ Text	☑ Text
❏	❏	❏	❏
❏	❏	❏	❏
❏	❏	❏	❏
❏	❏	❏	❏
❏	❏	❏	❏
❏	❏	❏	❏
❏	❏	❏	❏
❏	❏	❏	❏
❏	❏	❏	❏
min.	*min.*	*min.*	*min.*

ENDNOTES

Introduction

1. Rabbi Hayim Halevy Donin, *To Be a Jew* (New York: Basic Books, Inc., 1972), pp. 159-160.
2. Ibid.
3. Ibid.
4. Owen Chadwick, ed., *The Library of Christian Classics: Western Asceticism* (Philadelphia: The Westminster Press, 1963), n.p.
5. *Strong's Greek-Hebrew Dictionary*, PC Study Bible ed., s.v. "meditate."
6. *The International Standard Bible Encylopaedia*, PC Study Bible ed., s.v. "meditate."

Section One—Theophanies

1. Peter R. Carrell, *Jesus and the Angels: Angelology and the Christology of the Apocalypse of John* (New York: Cambridge University Press, 1997), p. 38.

Section Two—The Psalms

1. *The International Standard Bible Encylopaedia*, PC Study Bible ed., s.v. "the Psalms."

Section Four—The Song of Songs

1. Fr. Juan G. Arintero, O.P., *The Song of Songs: A Mystical Exposition*, trans. James Valendar, M.A. and Jose L. Morales, Ph.D. (Rockford, Illinois: Tan Books and Publishers, Inc., 1992), p. 7.

Section Six—The Prayers of Jesus

1. Evelyn Underhill, *The Cloud of Unknowing* (London: John M. Watkins, 1922), n.p.
2. M. Basil Pennington, O.C.S.O., *Centering Prayer: Renewing an Ancient Christian Prayer Form* (Garden City, NY: Doubleday and Company, Inc., 1980), p. 62.
3. Helen Bacovcin, trans., *The Way of a Pilgrim: A Classic of Orthodox Spirituality* (New York: Image Books, 1978), pp. 23-24.
4. E. Kadloubovsky and G. E. H. Palmer, trans., *The Philokalia* (London: Faber and Faber, 1983), p. 74.

Section Seven—Apostolic Prayers

1. Mike Bickle, "Web Site Notes on the Apostolic Prayers," *Friends of the Bridegroom*, 1998. http://www.fotb.com/ (accessed fall 2001).

Other Books by Wesley Campbell

Welcoming a Visitation of the Holy Spirit
by Wesley Campbell

In Welcoming a Visitation of the Holy Spirit, Wesley Campbell takes a refreshing look at the renewal movement known as the Toronto Blessing. He combines the expertise of a biblical scholar with the unabashed enthusiasm of someone who's fallen in love with his Savior all over again.

Learn about:
• Prophecies in 1984 that pointed to events in Toronto in 1994
• Biblical tests you can use to identify a visitation of the Holy Spirit
• The spiritual meanings behind falling down, shaking, and laughing
• New outbreaks of renewal and the future of the movement

Other Books currently in progress

The Radical Army
Revival & Social Justice: A Paradigm of End-Time Harvest
by Wesley Campbell & Stephen Court

The harvest at the end of the age will come through dramatic sweeps of God's power and the application of social justice to the world.

The Supernatural Hero Series

Historical, biographical, inspirational and supernatural! Read about God's heroes of the past as they brought God's rule to the earth.
• The Martyrs: Perpetua & Felicity
• The Life of St. Patrick
• Martin of Tours
• St. Columba of Iona
• Celtic Heroines of the Church
Proposed 10 -15 volumes in the series

PRAYING THE BIBLE SERIES:
OTHER RESOURCES RELATED TO
THE BOOK OF PRAYERS

We would like to offer these additional resources for you to listen to, and use in your own personal prayer and devotional times. These CD's are directly associated with certain genres contained within The Book of Prayers.

Prayers from the Desert
Praying the Psalms with Wesley Campbell
"Prayers from the Desert" focuses specifically on praying the Psalms in a context of original musical arrangements and accompaniment.
Prayers from the Desert available in CD, Cassette & Instrumental CD

Selah
Singing the Psalms with the Heather Clark Band
After having written the music for "X-treme Disciples" and "The Elijah Revolution" Heather became hooked on Praying the Bible. Taking it a step further she began to sing-pray the Psalms. "Selah: Singing the Psalms was the result. With impacting rhythms and lyrics straight from the word of God "Selah" has become a great favorite with the younger crowd.
Selah - Singing The Psalms available in CD

Psalms & Hymns Vol. 1
Praying with Wesley Campbell
Hebrew Psalms set to all new arrangements of Hymns. Join Wesley Campbell as he prays the word of God as it is written.
Psalms & Hymns Vol. 1 available in CD

Apostolic Prayers
Praying the Apostolic Prayers with Mike Bickle
With revival bursting upon us, this album will inspire you to better pray the revival prayers of the Apostle Paul.
Apostolic Prayers available in CD & Instrumental CD

The Fire of Love
Praying the Song of Songs with Mike Bickle
"Many waters cannot quench love... it burns like a blazing fire, the very flame of the Lord."
This prophetic love song is also accompanied by an original musical soundtrack.
Fire Of Love available in CD, Cassette & Instrumental CD

Dark Yet Lovely
Sung by Heather Clark
This CD tells the story of the Song of Songs. These intimate and passionate songs display the love relationship between the Bride and Bridegroom.
Dark Yet Lovely available in CD

The Bride's Anthem
Praying the Adoring Prayers from Revelations with Mike Bickle
Mike Bickle prays the visions of the Apostle John from the perspective of the adoring Bride waiting for her soon coming Bridegroom.
Music by Darryl Taylor The Bride's Anthem available in CD & Instrumental CD

TOLL FREE ORDERING: 1-888-738-4832
resources@prayingthebible.com
www.prayingthebible.com

OTHER PRAYER CD's IN
THE PRAYING THE BIBLE SERIES:

PTB 05: Prayers for the Harvest
PTB 07: Prayers for X-treme Disciples
PTB 11: Prayers For Israel

PTB 12: Prayers for the Elijah Revolution
PTB 15: Children's Prayer

REVIVAL NOW! WORSHIP CD SERIES:

RNW 02: Fireland: Cry of the Celts
RNW 03: Temple Dance
RNW 05: Cry Mercy

OTHER PRAYER RESOURCES IN
THE PRAYING THE BIBLE SERIES:

These paperback booklets are approximately 75 - 100 pages...

Book #1. Praying the Bible: The Pathway To Spirituality
This mini book is the first in the series that gives an indepth
explanation of the "Praying The Bible" concept.

OTHER BOOKS CURRENTLY IN PROGRESS

Book #2. What are you Praying When you Pray the Bible
This mini book will explore each of the eight particular prayer styles, showing a sample prayer
of each category, and describing how to pray them. This booklet will contain a complete list of
prayers, that belong to each of the seven categories of biblical prayers.

Book #3. Teaching Children to Pray the Bible
This is a book written to parents who want their children to pray. How do they do it? Most parents
do not feel effective in their own prayer life let alone, trying to teach their children how. How do
you teach your children to pray? What does a parent do? This booklet will explain the process
thoroughly, include sample prayers and a weekly check list. The mechanics of how children pray,
and how parents get their children to pray.

Book #4. Praying the Bible through the Ages
Praying the bible is not new. "Praying the Bible Through the Ages" is a fascinating history over-
view of how the greatest saints of all the ages have prayed to God by praying the Holy Scriptures.
This mini-book includes Hebrew Prayer, NT Prayer, The Prayer of the early Church Fathers and
Desert Fathers, Prayer East and West, Eastern Prayer, Benedictine Prayer, Celtic Prayer, The
'Lectio Divina' and Monastic Prayer, Bible Praying of the great revivalists and the modern prayer
movement.

Book #5. Praying The Bible and Revival
This fifth book in the series will explore the relationship between praying the bible and revival.

CONTACT INFORMATION

For Bookings and Information on Wesley & Stacey Campbell:

Be A Hero
Suite D225A - 2041 Harvey Avenue
Kelowna, BC. Canada
V1Y 6G7
Phone: (250) 717-1003
Fax: (250) 862-2942
E-mail: wesley@prayingthebible.com

Conferences & Schools:

Be A Hero along with New Life Church, host 4 to 6 conferences and 1 to 2 training & equipping schools per year in beautiful Kelowna, BC. If you would like to join us for any or all of these events, please contact us at the above address or check out our website at www.prayingthebible.com for more details.

Resources:

Toll Free Ordering: 1-888-738-4832
E-mail: resources@prayingthebible.com
www.prayingthebible.com